The Small-Engine
Handbook

The Small-Engine
Handbook

Peter Hunn

MOTORBOOKS

In memory of Walt Thomas III,
who always appreciated quick-starting small engines.

First published in 2005 by Motorbooks, an imprint of
MBI Publishing Company, Galtier Plaza, Suite 200,
380 Jackson Street, St. Paul, MN 55101-3885 USA

Motorbooks titles are also available at discounts in bulk
quantity for industrial or sales-promotional use. For
details write to Special Sales Manager at MBI Publishing
Company, Galtier Plaza, Suite 200, 380 Jackson Street,
St. Paul, MN 55101-3885 USA.

ISBN 0-7603-2049-7

Editorial: Dennis Pernu
Design: Christopher Fayers

Printed in China

About the author:
Peter Hunn was drawn
to small engines as a
kindergartner, when an
elderly neighbor with a
bad arm asked him to
try firing up the guy's
lawnmower. Three
determined pulls later,
that mower's rope-start
Briggs & Stratton
sputtered to life and
started Hunn noticing
other little air-cooled
engines, as well as
outboard motors, about
which he's authored
seven books. The former owner of several local radio
stations, Hunn teaches communication and broadcast
subjects at the State University of New York at Oswego,
and has served as a public school administrator. In that
role he always enjoys taking a moment to drop by the
mechanic tech shop, where kids learn about small-engine
operational theory and repair.

CONTENTS

INTRODUCTION

Though rather unlikely catalysts, 25 rusty pieces of toy-train track in a crumpled paper shopping bag caused me to write this book. That's because they served as trading stock for a three-way, sixth-grade playground swap in which one kid got the Lionel track, another acquired a battered BB gun, and I netted a "classic" 1955 power mower. Its modest two-stroke Clinton engine was reputed to "run great," but the mill's reputation became increasingly tarnished with every pull on the frayed starter cord. My father suggested cleaning the carburetor, an operation that occurred in a discarded chicken potpie plate half-filled with gasoline, and took me an entire Saturday to conduct. Several neighbors watched skeptically, predicting that the darn thing was hopelessly shot. For some serendipitous reason, however, the procedure proved successful enough for me to coax that little red Clinton to life and busily manicure the entire lawn.

Having "repaired" that formerly comatose motor earned me sufficient neighborhood kudos to hang out a "small-engine shop" shingle. A fellow 12-year-old motor nut and I went into the mower-service business under the hand-scribbled banner *Hunn & Schnabel Internal Combustion Engines*. Admittedly, we had only a couple of paying clients that long-ago summer, but we benefited from hours of experimenting with various and sundry small engines on worn-out mowers donated by folks too lazy to go to the dump. Some had seen us chugging along with a Radio Flyer wagon tied to an ancient reel-type self-propelled machine that we drove several miles to the local store and back. The slow and palsied jaunt gave us ample time to discuss the finer points of power-equipment and small-engine application, from lawn tractors to go-karts, over the *ratt-a-tatt-tatt* of the exhaust.

Over the years, I've dragged home dozens of orphaned mowers, snowblowers, chainsaws, minibikes, karts, and the like that simply seemed to possess too much personality to be sentenced to some scrap heap. Their one-lung powerplants—with badges boasting fine American makers such

6

Clinton dubbed its two-cycle products "Panthers," though none looked nearly as ferocious as the little motors' big-cat namesake. This 2½-horse Clinton Panther VS-400-3105 is a bit more deluxe than my old mower's VS-200, though both would appear essentially the same to casual observers. The pictured mill has an additional ¾ horsepower and a rewind starter with a roller that allows for efficiently pulling the cord at angles from straight out to straight up. Both motors hail from the 1950s and sport the "red heat-resisting enamel" and arrowhead logo that typically identified this Iowa-built brand. Clinton brochures from the Eisenhower era indicate their little two-strokers were also available in "dark green, or other colors upon special order."

as Briggs & Stratton, Lawn Boy, McCulloch, Tecumseh, and West Bend—often prompted me to delve into company histories, so that vintages and model specifications could be discovered.

Along the way, I've found out that others share the easily entered small-engine hobby. *The Small-Engine Handbook* is designed to make identifying and fixing up or restoring old single-cylinder, air-cooled motors more fun. In these colorful pages, any enthusiast can take a brief historical trip into the worlds of more than 30 small-engine

manufacturers, get a working understanding of small-engine operating principles, learn how to set up a useful home-based small-engine shop, and walk through several repair/restoration cases. Best of all, putting the *Handbook* into practice may yield inexpensive pleasure. The case studies can be replicated by anyone—or any parent/child team—with a small-engine-powered machine rescued from the dump or picked up for a few bucks on eBay or at a yard sale. No doubt, your revitalized small engine will bring true satisfaction when it's put back to work.

CHAPTER 1
BRIEF HISTORY
OF SMALL ENGINES

Start a collection of castaway or vintage single-cylinder motors and some observer is bound to ask which one is the oldest. While many small-engine buffs tinker with motors manufactured four or five decades ago, even they might be amazed to discover that the first internal combustion engines began busily sputtering away in the middle of the nineteenth century. The basis for the genre was laid around 1860, when a French waiter decided he'd rather be an inventor than serve croissants. One of Jean Joseph Etienne Lenoir's creations was an engine fired via battery ignition on illuminating gas piped into his Paris workshop. Reliable sources like Grayson's *Beautiful Engines* call Lenoir's 8-foot-long, 1,768-pound machine the first relatively "practical engine that used something other than steam and solid fuel to do work." Even so, Lenoir's 1-horsepower, water-cooled unit would hardly be recognizable as the great-grandfather to millions of offspring mounted on power mowers, chainsaws, weed whackers, generators, or go-karts.

When forming a definition of *small engine*—that is to say, an air-cooled, one-cylinder motor of less than 20-ci piston displacement, light enough to be lifted by one person and designed to power a variety of applications—motorcycle powerplants of the early 1900s provide a firm historical foundation. Derivatives of these lightweight mills found themselves refined and adapted to many military, industrial, and even some household uses (particularly on washing machines) during, as well as between, the World Wars. After 1945, with very little fanfare, colorful little engines from the likes of Briggs & Stratton, Clinton, and Lauson were elevated to icons of modern suburban living.

NEARLY A FULL HALF-ACRE TO MOW!

The call by English high society for well-manicured estate lawns motivated a Mr. Edwin Budding of Gloucestershire to patent his idea for a mechanical grass cutter. Its spiraling blades, placed parallel to the ground, chopped all upright

Some of the earliest domestic users of small engines were folks doing laundry with a gas-powered washing machine. Maytag is the best-remembered appliance maker to produce both pioneer washers and reliable small engines. This foot-started, ¾-horsepower Maytag was liberated from its washing machine so that it could show off for attendees of a vintage tractor meet. It's a great example of what engine buffs call a "runner," meaning the motor isn't beautifully restored, but operates very well and can be used without fear of scratching up the paint.

grass that came between them and a carefully aligned "bed-plate." This 1830 invention would look familiar to fans of the reel-type lawnmowers used by diehards with small, flat yards, and reminiscent of the huge gang mowers that some golf course maintenance crews tow behind a tractor. From the early twentieth century through the mid-1950s, self-propelled versions of the reel mower—typically powered by a one-lung, air-cooled engine—were signs of good lawn care. But in a bumpy yard featuring a few stray sticks, rocks, or wind-blown items, the reel cutting mechanism could be easily frustrated or damaged.

My very first adventure in power mowing serves as an

The Briggs & Stratton–powered Simplicity walk-behind tractor is the manufacturer's early edition, fitted with a reel-type mower. Because such tractors and related attachments could cut grass, till soil, pull a small wagon, and plow snow, they were especially popular with hobby farmers.

Warrensburg, Missouri's Goodall Manufacturing Corporation held the U.S. patent for direct-drive vertical power lawnmowers. A specially designed Lauson four-stroker enlivened the 1948 Goodall advertised here. It was promoted as being able to cut "any height grass or tough weeds in 1/3rd time" of nonpowered, reel-style push mowers. Though the brand is arguably the true grandfather of every direct-drive rotary lawnmower in existence, Goodall has long faded from the scene, and surviving examples are rare today. It's interesting to note that while Goodall advertised far and wide for dealers willing to take on his product, offspring of the original direct-drive rotary mower are now routinely sold in venues as then unimaginable as the front lobbies of grocery stores.

Only five horses from a 1950s Briggs & Stratton horizontal-shaft engine are needed to move this cute, nicely restored Bantam tractor around the barnyard.

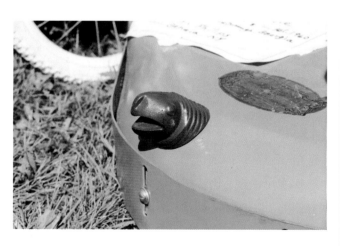

Some mower makers tried tackling the growing post–World War II rotary-mower market by belt-driving the blade with a horizontal-shaft engine. This machine from McDonough Power Equipment of McDonough, Georgia, is a forerunner of the Snapper lawn and snowblower line. That 8-horsepower Briggs & Stratton mill with cast-iron cylinder bore and I/C (integrated circuit) electronic ignition is a replacement engine. Dig that crazy "snapper" turtle hood ornament!

example. At six years old and barely able to see above the mower's handles, I ran over a wayward shirt that some gust had set free from the neighbor's clothesline. The tangle tightly twisted whatever was left of the unfortunate apparel into and around the blades and then choked the little Briggs & Stratton horse-and-a-half, rope-start motor to a sickening halt. Similar encounters with stones, the sole of an old shoe, and pieces of wire necessitated blade resharpening and realignment, and finally netted me a new kind of mower that cut through practically any challenge a suburban yard could offer. Having sold the old reel machine to a teen who'd coveted its engine for some homebrew go-kart, my dad came home from the local hardware store with a bright orange rotary lawnmower enlivened by a 2½-horsepower,

ONE MAN PORTABLE GASOLINE SAW:

This 20" one man saw may be converted to a two man saw by the addition of a helper's end at slight additional cost. One man saw — weight 52 lbs., Price $325.00 f. o. b. factory.

Notching for directional felling.

Completing the back cut — Timber!

Reed-Prentice Corporation of Worcester, Massachusetts, helped modernize the logging industry in 1946 with its one-man portable Timberhog gasoline saw. At $325, however, the Timberhog cost as much as a decent used car. Los Angeles–based McCulloch supplied the two-stroke (4-horsepower at 4,500 rpm) engines for the 52-pound machines and used lightweight diecast aluminum and magnesium to fabricate the motors. When the California company felt confident that it could offer an even lighter engine than the ones designed for Reed-Prentice, McCulloch decided to enter the chainsaw business under its own brand name.

four-stroke motor with rewind starting. Nearly every weekend, this happy single-cylinder machine joined the chorus of a dozen other such devices busily humming away on most every piece of property in our neighborhood.

Leonard B. Goodall of Warrensburg, Missouri, is said to have invented the rotary power mower in 1939. His concept was simple enough: Attach a blade to the business end of a vertical crankshaft engine, mount the motor on a rolling deck that gets pushed with a handle, and let the mower whip through anything in its path. Rotaries caught on fast. Though arguably more effective than their reel-style sisters, rotary mowers require far fewer parts. Consequently, modest early rotary models could be had for 75 percent less than the price of some reel-type power mowers of similar cutting

Some buffs say that small engines were given their most interesting venue in tiny bulldozers. The red-bladed Lennox Kitty Track 600 gets its go from a rope-start Briggs. It hails from a Des Moines, Iowa, factory and steers with traditional dozer levers.

ENGINES, ENGINES EVERYWHERE!

Tell someone how many small engines there are in the world and they'll likely admonish you a trillion billion times never to exaggerate. Truth is, anybody on even a casual quest for a preowned, one-lung mill in the free-to-$50 range probably doesn't possess enough storage space to extend the search for more than a few days. When you're browsing the graveyard of a power-equipment shop, stopping at a lawn sale, checking out the bargain classified ads in your local "penny saver" paper, surfing online auctions, or keeping an eye peeled for a discarded mower on trash day, there's no need to feel desperate and take just any old thing. Instead, have some fun by being a bit discriminating. Unless you're seeking one of the uncommon brands highlighted in Chapter 2, pass by any motor that's stuck, rusty, corroded, or missing parts. The used small-engine supply is like water in the Mighty Mississippi—it just keeps rolling along. There are too many complete small engines hoping to be adopted for you to try saving the ones that have been horribly neglected or cannibalized. Given the chance, though, take a "parts" engine to serve as a donor for the mill you'll be revitalizing. Be sure it's the same model or has appropriately interchangeable components.

Small engines are indeed *small*, so they can be hiding almost anywhere. On a hunch, one Northwestern buff contacted a modest manufacturing company that, in the 1960s, used to build light industrial machines powered by Clinton motors. His chance call to this firm netted the collector a shipment of new-old-stock Model A-500 kart engines that had been stacked in a corner of the company's storage room for decades. Don't be surprised to find that the small-engine hunt is a big part of the hobby's fun!

For small-engine enthusiasts hoping to find a needed part, the best power-equipment repair shops are the ones with so much "preowned" inventory and so little time and space to organize it that they'll let willing customers have the enjoyable task of rummaging through all their stuff. Often, such a search leads to neat things that you didn't even know you were looking for.

When the UPS deliveryman finished unloading this shipment of "forgotten" new-old-stock motors, the collector who had tracked them down in a Midwest warehouse counted seven complete Clinton A-500 kart engines and a couple of parts motors. None had ever been run.

width. In unison with the countless housing developments springing up throughout the United States and Canada beginning during the late 1940s, hundreds of rotary mower brands appeared on the scene to satisfy consumer demand for quick and easy yard manicuring. In 1971, as a chronological example, nearly 5 million rotary mowers were sold in the United States, placing the total in American garages and backyard sheds that year at about 40 million. Though that's accounted for lots of small engines through the years, it is dwarfed by contemporary numbers.

For many future motorheads whose weekly allowance was tied to cutting the grass, experience with the family power mower's engine provided them with their first motorized experience and made related lawn chores seem almost fun. One manufacturer suggested to parents of teens, "When Junior asks to borrow the family car, let him

Considered a pioneer in American chainsaw development, the Kiekhaefer Corporation original maker of Mercury Outboards— was into compact and lightweight, but rugged, chainsaw engines in a big way from the World War II years until 1953. That year, Kiekhaefer suddenly decided to cut its relationship with the Disston saw folks, who actually marketed units like this 38-pound 1950 version (with the its chain riding over the outer edges of the chain bar).

It's Easier With a New

McCULLOCH MAC/35A

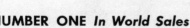

NUMBER ONE *In World Sales*

★ High-speed gear-drive cutting. 4.22 to 1 gear ratio gives plenty of lugging power.

★ Weighs only 20 pounds — lightest gear-drive saw made.

★ Starts fast — goes into action fast — when you want it to. Points and coil are weather-proofed to assure fast starting in winter and summer.

★ Torture-tests prove dependability.

★ Cuts flush with the ground.

★ Thrifty to buy, thrifty to operate — a real chain saw bargain.

★ McCulloch new Super Pintail® chain — the smoothest cutting, longest lasting chain on the market.

★ Diaphragm carburetor enables you to cut in any position, even when saw is upside down.

★ Takes bars up to 32", 15" Plunge Bow, 24" Paddle Bow, All Purpose Drill and Brushcutter attachments.

See Your McCulloch Dealer For a Mac/35A Demonstration

BULLETIN ADV-701-5/60

LITHO IN U.S.A.

By 1960, McCulloch could routinely produce affordable chainsaw engines in the 20-pound range. Models like the one serving this MAC 35A, or better yet, the more compact 1-41 and Super 55A, not only made the company a leader in the saw industry, but go kart fanatics interested in using the high-revving McCulloch motors in their speedy little vehicles.

VERY SMALL ENGINES

To satisfy detail-oriented readers who'd correctly remind me that vintage model engines technically fit this book's coverage criteria (single-cylinder, air-cooled, gasoline-fired motor of less than 20-ci piston displacement), an example of the diminutive genre is noted here. Often dubbed by model power buffs as "spark ignition engines," these minimills began appearing after World War I in model airplanes, cars, and boats. The golden age of model ignition engines ran from the mid-1930s to about 1949, when the simpler "glow plug" model engine format began to quickly usurp the traditional miniature motors' thunder—or buzz. While glow (or "glo") engines, with their diesel-like glow plug, require only a battery to heat the plug during initial startup, model ignition engines utilize a coil, condenser, batteries for spark, ignition points, an ignition timer, and a tiny spark plug. To facilitate the hobby, makers like Champion, AC, Autolite, and lesser-known brands each offered a line of spark plugs that could be dwarfed by a coin.

With few exceptions, the little engines that those plugs fit were two-strokers that sipped a gas/oil mixture often blended in a jar and introduced to the fuel tank via a medicine dropper. By the early 1950s, several hundred manufacturers had marketed model spark-ignition engines. Because many such firms were obscure—perhaps having only advertised their wares to a crowded model marketplace in a single issue of some hobby magazine before going out of business—their engines are considered quite collectable today. That means that most are now retired to the display case, but some of the nicely designed and more common examples (such as a late-1940s Ohlsson & Rice "23" or Herkimer Tool & Model Works' Super 60) still compete in vintage-style model events.

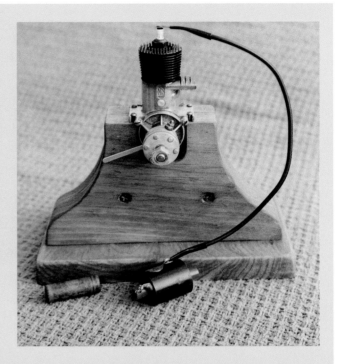

Shown with ignition coil and condenser, the 1946 Ohlsson & Rice .23-ci air-cooled single certainly qualifies as a small engine. This brand was noted for its excellent running qualities at reasonable ($16.50 for the model shown) prices.

A dismantled 1947 Thor shows signs of piston "scuffing," a remarkable condition for an entry-level model spark-ignition engine brand now fondly remembered for seldom starting. The .29-ci motor weighed in at 4.5 ounces and was offered by a New York hobby shop to mail-order customers. For $6.95 circa 1948 (and later less), the Thor was sold in kit form. Decades after the last factory-produced one was mailed to some naïvely overoptimistic modeler, a collector had a chance to rummage through the cellar of the defunct hobby store that sold Thors and came across several 55-gallon oil drums filled with never-used Thor crankcases, cylinders, and pistons. (For point of reference, the Thor piston is only about ¾ inch tall.)

drive a Moto-Mower!" It was often while trying to motivate a stubborn mower mill to start or run more smoothly that youngsters learned basic principles of small-engine operation and discovered that their motor had a particular personality. Add a patient adult, a pair of pliers, screwdriver, adjustable wrench, some newspaper (on which to put the tiny carburetor parts), plus a carefree Saturday morning to the aforementioned mechanical diagnostic session, and we're talking a memorable parent/child experience.

THROW AWAY THE AXE!

If I handled the old hatchet in our garage carefully, I was allowed to chop some kindling for the fireplace. The chainsaw, however, was strictly off-limits until I became a more experienced woodsman. Truth be told, that early-1950s vintage saw was too heavy for me to tote anyway. It was the cutter's high-revving (when we could keep it going) two-stroke that really interested me. The following autumn, when we got a newer, lighter version, the salesman only offered five bucks for trade-in of the old one, so I was given the engine to take apart. Most of its intricate pieces are probably still waiting in a coffee can somewhere.

No one is completely sure who invented the chainsaw. There are references to a chain-blade saw being used as early as 1905 by a now-unknown outdoorsman in Northern California. Rather than an air-cooled engine, though, a marine motor powered his machine. It was probably water-cooled, thus limiting its portability and increasing the unit's weight to the point where several loggers were required. Modern chainsaws' more direct lineage can be traced to Germany, where Andreas Stihl received a 1929 patent for his "hand held mobile chainsaw designed for woodcutting." Actually, this rig required two pairs of hands: one person to hold up the engine section and another to grasp a hefty handle at the end of the saw's long blade.

In early spring 1941, the U.S. Army got hold of a Stihl chainsaw that had been smuggled out of World War II Germany. American military officials gave word that they wanted someone in the States to make a similar "chain timber saw" for use by U.S. troops who might soon be called upon to rip through trees or to cut lumber on or around the battlefield. The then-fledgling company that manufactured Mercury outboard motors borrowed the contraband Stihl, studied it, and developed a two-cylinder Merc chainsaw engine that bested the German motor in power, ruggedness, ease of operation, and lightness. Like the Stihl, it was fitted to a long blade bar/chain for dual-man use. After the war, Mercury introduced a 38-pound single-cylinder one-man saw that helped set the standard for the millions of chainsaws that have followed. The McCulloch Corporation also

REO used a crank-start Briggs to power its early-1960s attempt at selling single-stage snowblowers to a public that was still not very familiar with such machines.

served as an industry pioneer, when it produced saw engines featuring featherweight magnesium castings. Companies like Poulan and Homelite also worked overtime making saw engines lighter and more reliable. As millions of acres across the country were cleared for new housing, the chainsaw engine became a familiar sound of progress. Their feisty motors helped make wood chips fly like snow on a northern February night.

PERSONAL BLIZZARD BUSTERS

Cold images of tall, white drifts came to Arthur Sicard's inventive mind when the Quebec resident happened to see a farm thresher making quick work of a field of wheat. As he watched the wheat get churned into the mechanism and thrown out of a chute and onto a wagon, Sicard figured a similar rotary blade arrangement could eat up snow that was plugging up roads and then blow the stuff out of the way. Mounted on the front of a truck, Sicard's resulting "snow remover snowblower" started keeping Montreal

A direct competitor to chainsaws was this 1958 Wright Super Rebel reciprocating cutter. The scabbard under the blade bar shadows the Wright's sharp teeth, which move back and forth (like a manual handsaw) when the modified Power Products two-stroke engine is running.

streets free of accumulated snow in the mid-1920s. It provided a basis for scores of companies that have marketed much smaller domestic walk-behind snowblowers, reportedly starting with a Toro unit in 1951. Small engines comprise a major component of snowblowing, and after an early-1970s snowblower industry shakedown—during which a flurry of minor snowblower makers left the business—Tecumseh and Briggs & Stratton motors specially designed for cold-weather operation power most of today's ever-growing legion of snowblowers.

HEY KIDS! WE'VE GOT MOTORS FOR YOUR KART OR MINIBIKE!

Huge numbers of baby boomers provided a potential market for a little Omaha, Nebraska, company infamous for placing 1x2-inch ads in the back of 1960s *Popular Science*–type magazines. "KIDS!" the advertisements screamed, "Learn how you can buy used engines for $15 and up, new engines for $30. Send for free confidential list and engine deal coupons!" With many young people presently devoted to video screens, it may seem odd that anyone would think that kids could be enticed to buy a cheap secondhand, one-lung motor, but lots of them craved such power to enliven a minibike or go-kart frame. Having a working vehicle of either aforementioned variety during the late 1950s through the 1970s was indeed a bona fide juvenile status symbol and even a blast for older teens and parents to pilot. Mimicking the motors that fueled this

phenomenon, beginning in 1963 Mattel marketed a plastic, fake air-cooled single designed to look and sound like a real engine. Mounting hardware was included so that kids could use the Mattel *"V-RROOM!"* pseudo mill on bicycles, tricycles, or pushcarts. A pair of D-size flashlight batteries helped produce the idle to high-revving motor noises that gave youngsters at least a sense of being in control of a small internal combustion powerplant.

Pioneer minibike development can be assigned to lots of long-since forgotten farmers and hunters who modified junked bicycle frames to roll on small, fat wheelbarrow tires and then fit their "power trail bikes" with a retired lawnmower engine. By the early 1960s, *Science & Mechanics* magazine offered do-it-yourselfers plans for "Beats Walkin'," a "tote-all scooter made with an old bike frame and a used one-lung engine . . . for [grownups] and the kids to zip around on." The widely sold directions showed how to make Beats Walkin' into "a high-power/high-ratio sports version for off the road use, or a fast street job . . . that'll go about 26 mph with a 2½ or 3 hp, 4-cycle engine." It became the blueprint for the classic minibike design offered by firms like Bird Engineering and copied by tiny companies such as the previously mentioned outfit hoping to sell its $2 "step-by-step details" on minibike and go-kart construction by throwing in those free tips on securing $15 motors.

Though the first go-karts arguably can be traced to homemade soapbox cars of the 1920s, the official genre has a more specific originator than does the minibike. In 1956,

MAKE A SPARK TESTER FOR A BUCK OR LESS

There's not much to this tool, but it'll sure come in handy when you're wondering if a magneto has fire. To construct a quick and easy spark tester, get a battery clip of at least 4 inches in length. The clamp from a decommissioned set of jumper cables is ideal. Find an old spark plug that you know works well. (Not sure? Well, you can always check it on the tester.) Next, use a hose clamp to secure the plug to the clip. After attaching the spark plug to the test engine's mag wire and grounding the clip to a metal surface on the crankcase, spin the flywheel (pull the starter cord) and watch for spark in the plug's bottom. The more robust and regular the spark, the better the magneto's (or "mag's") components. Hearing a little electrical "snap" down in the plug gap is a good sign, too. It's typically best that there's no spark plug in the plug hole when conducting tests. Otherwise, you'll be cranking against compression. Perhaps the most important mag fact to remember is that you can damage a magneto coil and condenser by spinning the flywheel without grounding the spark plug wire to the crankcase or attaching it to a spark plug that is threaded into its hole or on a tester clamped to the engine.

SNOW BLOWER BOB-CAT GRASS MOWER

SAVES TIME Opens up blocked driveways and walks in minutes instead of hours. Savings in time, comfort and convenience will pay for the Bob-Cat quickly.

SAVES WORK Gone forever are the back-breaking hours of laborious work for you and your family. Snow is discharged a considerable distance, tending to prevent cleared areas drifting shut again.

SAVES HEALTH Prevents heart-strain due to over-exertion. Shoveling snow and mowing grass are two of the most energy consuming, muscle taxing jobs. Let a Bob-Cat prolong your life.

COMPARE THESE FEATURES

- 3 Forward Speeds and Neutral
- Multiple Disc Clutch
- No-Load Starting
- Clears 20" Path
- Handles 12" Depth
- Positive Rotary Action
- Handles Wet and Dry Snow
- Right or Left Discharge
- Adjustable Discharge Distance
- Better Balanced
- Easily Handled
- Simple and Safe

Because the Bob-Cat was specifically designed as a snow removal unit, it incorporates features such as better balance, easier handling and proper travel speed range, which provide superior performance. Its exclusive, positive feeder mechanism pulls snow into the machine — enabling it to handle all types of snow from a thin fluffy texture to heavy wet, with full effectiveness.

It is ruggedly built to withstand severe service, yet is perfectly balanced to provide maximum traction with complete handling ease, enabling a woman or youngster to operate it.

The Bob-Cat is equipped with a three speed transmission, enabling you to adjust the forward travel speed to the exact snow conditions encountered. It will whirl its way through banks 12" and over and clean a 20" swath down to the surface. The snow discharge can be directed either to the right or left, and the discharge distance can also be regulated as desired.

The Bob-Cat has been thoroughly tested in many sections of the snow belt and the experience thus gained has resulted in better design, better construction and far superior performance in all type of snow conditions.

Quickly Convertible To Rotary Mower

A 20" rotary mower attachment quickly converts the Bob-Cat into a powerful lawn mower. Wheels are set so machine will trim within 1" on the side. Large front wheels assure easy rolling and maneuvering. The mower is encased in a heavy steel frame for extra rigidity, strength and permanent alignment. A riding sulky can be attached, which together with the three speed transmission enables the Bob-Cat to provide complete mowing convenience.

WISCONSIN MARINE CO.
PEWAUKEE, WISCONSIN

For companies willing to take a chance in the fledgling snowblower marketplace, the late 1950s and early 1960s provided lots of wide-open territory. Typical of the era's snowblower brochures is this flyer for the Bob-Cat snowblower/lawnmower "convertible" in which a good deal of space is devoted to an explanation of how a snowblower works and why northerners should want one. Note Bob-Cat's dual snow-discharge chutes (only one at a time is utilized) instead of a rotating chute. That engine is a rope-start Briggs 8R6 with just 2½ horsepower.

Though most subscribers were knee-deep in snow, Science & Mechanics *devoted its February 1965 cover story to what many then termed the "bug craze," a warm-weather foray into minibikes, karts, and any other type of transportation utilizing one-lung, air-cooled "lawnmower engine" power. Volkswagens usurped the "bug" nickname shortly thereafter, but having fun in two-, three-, or four-wheeled vehicles with single-cylinder motors showed no signs of yielding.*

A summer 1959 ad from the first company to offer complete karts . . . the same outfit that legally owned the "Go Kart" name. Consequently, competitors like Fox of Janesville, Wisconsin—reportedly the earliest kart maker to truly mass-produce the little vehicles—skirted the coveted trademark by coining other descriptive names for their wares. Fox karts, for example, were dubbed "Go-Boy Carts" with a "C" instead of a "K." After Go Kart Manufacturing Company folded, Fox acquired the coveted nomenclature.

Art Ingels, who worked with a Southern California company that built Indianapolis 500 racing cars, came across a great-running 2½-horse West Bend two-stroke engine commandeered from a failed lawnmower venture. To put it to use, he welded up a tubular framework strong enough to hold the motor, a steering wheel, a modestly upholstered seat, and himself. Once the little chassis was fabricated, Ingels fitted its rear axle and front turning mechanism with chubby tires just high enough to keep his bodyless "kart" about 4 inches off of the ground. The West Bend drove a rear wheel via some sprockets and bike chain. Ingels' kart was off and running at about 30 miles per hour, which felt a lot faster so close to the surface of the parking lots and tennis courts where he ran it. Every time he whizzed around in the little vehicle, passersby asked where they could buy

one. The following June, Los Angeles–area businessman Bill Rowles spied Ingels' kart and established a partnership with two muffler-shop owners who figured folks would buy ready-to-run as well as weld-it-yourself versions of the Ingels creation. Rowles, Roy Desbrow, and Duffy Livingstone used the welding acumen of the latter pair's muffler establishment to start their Go Kart Manufacturing Company. Shortly thereafter, Ingels opened a kart-manufacturing concern (Caretta) that was quickly followed by several dozen makers vying for a profitable position in the Kennedy-era karting kraze.

Along with West Bend, three other small-engine makers played major roles in powering this go-kart (and minibike) mania. Power Products' simple and easy-to-work-on two-cycle jobs were quickly adopted by many buffs. Clinton, the

Sharing a neglected existence with many other old karts prior to today's baby boomer–driven acquisition frenzy, this 1962 Kavalla Kart spent many engineless years "up on blocks" in a basement before being marketed as "vintage" and quickly finding a new home. Its kitty driver would probably prefer the kart to remain a cat bed, but restoration and a souped-up engine are in the new owner's plans.

By the early 1970s, mini-biking had so captured the imagination of young Americans that even established power-equipment firms jumped in to capitalize on the phenomenon. Here's Allis-Chalmers' contribution to the genre. It's powered by a 5-horse Tecumseh.

Imagine being a young karting enthusiast and arriving home from school on your birthday to see a Clinton engine box ready for you to open! Looks like the giver has already inspected the merchandise. Flip open the carton, and there it is: a freshly factory-painted, bright-red Clinton A-500 kart motor! Hopefully Mom and Dad will let you attach it to that kart in the garage before announcing it's time to come indoors for ice cream and cake.

INTERESTING APPLICATIONS

Ask a game-show contestant to rattle off two things that small gasoline engines power and you'd probably not hear "washing machine and wheelbarrow." Though "lawnmower, chainsaw, garden tractor," and maybe even "leaf blower" would quickly come to most folks' minds, over the years, scores of other small-engine uses have made many chores a lot easier and recreational pursuits more fun. Here is a sampling of some interesting applications.

For chugging heavy loads over hill and dale, on rubble or rough terrain, there's the Clinton-fired power wheelbarrow by the Arrow Company. The Maytag single agitates a washing machine via pulleys and belts. That clever homemade faux "'32 Ford" hot rod is rear wheel–driven by a garden-variety Briggs & Stratton horizontal-shaft motor. Another Briggs pulls a "farmette touring" sulky in a three-wheel format. With its body high off those aggressive tires is a low-production, circa-1980 Spence Quadractor enlivened by an 8-horse Briggs & Stratton single. Sold through *Mother Earth News* as an environmentally friendly way to tour one's woods, the Spence had mechanically operated all-wheel steering via floor pedals. The steering wheel was stationary and only meant as something to hold onto while bouncing through the countryside. Prior to the karting era, Clinton four-stroke engines powered the Bennet Play Car and what might be considered the most elementary motorized four-wheeled vehicle ever: the Junior Hot Rod. It was marketed in the mid-1950s by an outfit that mated a one-lung Clinton to a bracket on the end of a little red wagon. Seems like it'd be a great rod for doing wheelies, even if involuntarily!

As was the case in the early 1950s when this Power Products two-stroke vertical-shaft mill was poised to tackle tall backyard weeds in a publicity shot, most small-engine output is still a province of the insatiable rotary-mower market.

Iowa company that supplied inexpensive two-strokes to Go Kart Manufacturing, made a name for itself in the kart community by offering ever-hotter versions of its reasonably priced basic motors. (Though not always specifically identified, Clintons were the main mills touted in the ubiquitous "HEY KIDS! CHEAP ENGINES!" ads.)

Veteran karters probably remember McCulloch as the most aggressive small-engine company. It was McCulloch whose mid-1950s rotary mower foray flopped, resulting in the West Bend Model 750 engines that powered them to be tossed into the surplus marketplace. It was one of those engines that Art Ingels used on his debut kart. When McCulloch witnessed the karting boom, it jumped into the sport by not only marketing high-rpm engines adapted from the MAC chainsaw line of its own manufacture, the Los Angeles firm also offered high-quality karts under the McCulloch brand. Though these and the earlier-noted West Bend, Power Products, and Clinton engines developed primarily for competition kart purposes saw action in sanctioned events, the majority of North American go-kart (and minibike) exploits were the province of relatively sleepy suburban or rural thoroughfares. Here, a couple of younger kids usually got assigned to watch for the cops while oily old four-cycle former mower engines powered unlicensed karts and minibikes.

Whether powering a hot kart, pokey mower, or any of at least a dozen other uses, small engines have touched the lives of millions of people. And it's a relationship that shows little sign of cooling down.

REO Trollabout

Converts any Rowboat up to 18'
INTO A TROLLER . . . RUNABOUT . . . UTILITY BOAT

Only
$99⁵⁰*
Model MKG-1
for fresh water only
F.O.B. Lansing, Mich.

Out of the way . . . won't interfere with trolling or casting . . Can't be lost overboard . . . pilfer-proof . . For fresh or salt water trolling

Trolls smoothly, quietly at speeds as low as ½ mph, up to 7 mph. Safe, seaworthy, maneuverable . . . ideal runabout for kids

Famous Reo 1¾ hp, 4-cycle Easy Starting Engine with Automatic Rewind Starter . . . automotive type downdraft carburetion . . . aluminum piston . . . air cooled . . . no water cooling system to clog and cause overheating . . . forward, neutral, reverse gears . . . 2-to-1 gear reduction for positive, purring power. Uses regular gas — no oil and gas to mix.

Here at last is the inboard trolling engine kit you need . . . at a price you can afford to pay! The Reo Trollabout Inboard Marine Engine ends backaches and blisters, gives you many hours of carefree enjoyment. Big, powerful Reo engine develops twice the thrust of outboard engine of same HP rating . . . makes your boat more stable and seaworthy. Trolls as slow as ½ mph, revs up to 7 mph to bring you back safely.

SPECIFICATIONS
Kit contains: Complete 1¾ HP Reo 4-cycle Easy Starting Engine. • Forward, neutral and reverse clutch. • Propeller shaft, couplings, brackets and mounts. • Rudder and steering cable. • Assorted pulleys, bolts, nuts, washers, etc. • Skeg bar and flexible exhaust extension available. • Model MKG1 for fresh water use, Model MKG11 for salt water use. • Net weight, 57 lbs.; shipping weight, 63 lbs.

* $124.50
— Model MKG
Salt or Fresh Wa

REO ENGINES
OVER 1,000,00
NOW IN USE

Kit comes complete, ready for installation with easy-to-follow instructions. Full-size template shows you exactly where to mount engine and drill holes.

If you can fix a leaky faucet, you can install a Reo Trollabout in as little as four hours with results that even a professional shipwright would be proud of. Only ordinary hand tools required — brace and bit, open-end wrenches, square and screwdriver.

REO MOTORS, INC., LAWN MOWER DIVISION, LANSING 20, MICHIGAN

During the early 1950s, several firms proved that small-engine owners didn't all have to be landlubbers. REO Motors' Lawn Mower Division marketed an inboard power kit called Trollabout that could be installed in rowboats for speeds between 1/2 and 7 miles per hour. The package included an air-cooled 1 3/4-horse REO four-stroker, forward-neutral-reverse clutch, propeller, prop shaft, rudder, steering cable, and assorted fittings. "If you can fix a leaky faucet," REO publicity promised, "you can install a REO Trollabout in as little as four hours with results that even a professional shipwright would be proud of." According to REO legend, however, a factory demonstrator Trollabout and associated flat-bottom rowboat sank during a publicity run. In all fairness to the little inboard, it had some satisfied customers, especially in calm waters where speed wasn't an issue. Imitators, like the Angler mini-inboards, used 2- and 3-horsepower Clinton power, while other competitors ran with Briggs & Stratton or Lauson four-cycle engines.

CHAPTER 2
SHORT PROFILES
OF MANUFACTURERS

On a snowy February evening in 1959, Ed Dague gave his wife a little kiss, slumped into a recliner, and told her it had been just another day down at the plant. "Nothing memorable," he said of his 8 to 4:30 shift on the small-engine assembly line. "It's not like I'm making history or anything." Had Mr. Dague realized, however, that someday the "old" motors he built would fascinate people, the Mid-westerner's mood might have been brighter that night.

This chapter is meant to pay tribute to the people who made the millions of motors that contribute to our rich mechanical history. It's also designed to satisfy some of the curiosity of those seeking background information on orphaned engines that have just found new homes. Admittedly, there aren't pages enough here for more than basic details. Even so, it is hoped that, whether consulting the sections on industry giants like Briggs & Stratton and Tecumseh, or the paragraph about the super-obscure Ekman kit motor, you'll get a sense that every small engine possesses an irresistible pedigree.

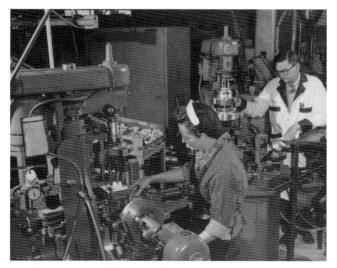

Could that be our own Ed Dague machining parts in this 1953 Lauson publicity still? Neither he nor his coworker look very joyful, but the small engines they helped produce certainly made a host of outdoor chores cheerier for thousands of folks. Courtesy Tecumseh Archives

BRIGGS & STRATTON

Shortly after Stephen Foster Briggs' 1907 graduation from South Dakota State College's engineering program, one of the school's sports coaches changed the young man's life with a single suggestion: "Why don't you meet a neighbor of mine, Harold Stratton, who might be interested in helping finance the production of that automobile motor you've designed?" The Briggs & Stratton Company quickly resulted and, along with it, a string of interesting but short-lived products, including several six-cylinder, two-stroke car engines and three autos that the duo hoped to mass-market under the brand name "The Superior." In 1910, the fledgling firm moved into the production of automotive electrical items, among them a simplified ignition system, voltage regulators, and switches.

Small engines entered the Milwaukee manufacturer's line in 1919, when it purchased the assets of an outfit that had some success building the Smith Motor Wheel, a ready-to-run powerplant-and-wheel arrangement that could be connected (like a big "training wheel") to the rear of one's bicycle for transformation into an instant motorbike. Briggs revamped his acquisition's 1½-horsepower Model C Motor Wheel with engineering improvements that netted the new Model D another ½ horsepower. This was the first small air-cooled mill to wear the Briggs & Stratton badge. In 1920, the company introduced a motor-only version of its Motor Wheel. Named the Type P (Portable), it had dual flywheels and moved the company into what would become its best-known product line. There'd be frequent introductions of improved models (such as an updated 1924 P) that even the most casual observer would recognize as a Briggs.

Through the 1920s, 1930s, and 1940s, offspring of this cast-iron engine were built in the Milwaukee factory and marketed for use powering everything from pumps, washing machines, and generators to saws, cement mixers, and lawnmowers. It was especially the latter application that made Briggs & Stratton a household brand by the early post–World War II era. By then, the company's name had become synonymous with small, horizontal-shafted, four-cycle motors constructed primarily of cast iron.

The Briggs & Stratton Motor Wheel gave the then-fledgling firm its initial success in the small-engine arena. The restored version in this photo should have a cylindrical gas tank mounted on a fender, which is also absent. Ads for the device were often targeted toward teens and possessed all of the early-1920s' innocent, flowery hyperbole that the advertising department could muster. "The fellow who owns a B&S Motor Wheel," the copy announced, "is to be envied, since he rides with no more effort than is required to steer the bicycle and to accelerate or retard the speed. It can be attached to any bicycle and provides power to speed over the roads at 25 miles an hour, yet it can be throttled down to maneuver carefully through the most congested traffic. Many hustling boys have made their Motor Wheel pay for itself in a very short time, as there are progressive merchants in every city, town, and village who will pay liberally for the services of a trusty boy with a Briggs & Stratton Motor Wheel. So write us a letter," the company requested, "and say, 'I am a boy who wants to know about the Motor Wheel,' and we will send you a dandy book, The Motor Wheel and Flyer. It's peachy!—and you can show it off to Dad. He will like the Motor Wheel Idea." By the way, that Flyer that the ad mentioned was a very basic two-passenger "buckboard" car with bicycle tires and Motor Wheel power. At 100 miles per gallon, those that were still around during the gas-rationing days of World War II were put back in service by drivers hoping to stretch their meager gasoline allotments.

Briggs & Stratton literature assigns 1948 as the pivotal year its engineering department began a program to move away from cast iron to the much lighter, but remarkably sturdy, diecast aluminum. Briggs' brass watched the rotary mower industry boom and understood that its four-strokes would have to be redesigned for lightness and compactness if they were to compete with the spate of featherweight two-cycle engines grabbing rotary market share. Briggs & Stratton made small-engine history in 1952 by cranking out nearly 1,016,000 motors that year. In 1954, the firm was granted a patent for the aluminum diecasting process its team developed. Like contemporary versions, the first lightweight diecast aluminum-alloy Briggs four-strokers, which debuted in vertical- and horizontal-shaft formats during the

An early-1960s 3-horse Briggs offers several interesting points to note. It's fitted with a crank-up "inertia" starter, which engine makers assumed would be widely accepted by a public who didn't like to pull a rope. On a particularly responsive engine, this feature was indeed convenient. Having to crank the thing more than several times, though, could really raise a temper. The inertia-release knob (protruding downward at right) that could lock the flywheel for cranking was another bugaboo. If the knob was twisted into the lock position while the motor ran, wow, what a terrifically noisy metallic muncher! This Briggs wears an "oil bath" air cleaner (secured by that wing nut). These units, which trapped dirt in the oily filter, were phased out as the 1960s progressed. In fact, seeing an engine with one is an indication of its age. Finally, the yellow B&S is notable because of its horizontal shaft in an increasingly rotary-shaft world. A motor like this wouldn't have been idle too long in any neighborhood filled with kids who had minibikes or karts on their minds.

The tag says Montgomery Wards, but it's a private brand washing machine engine built by Briggs & Stratton for the once-ubiquitous retailer. Identified as the model "WM," its foot starter would peek out of a shelf on the washer's support legs. The sideways spark plug allowed for adequate clearance, and that conduit hose could be hung out the laundry room window so whoever was doing the wash wouldn't be overcome by the exhaust.

**do it
the
easy
way
with a**

Homko
power mower

There's no better way to turn lawn work into play than with a HOMKO Power Mower. Powered by the finest, easy starting, nationally known, gas engine—sturdily built to give years of rugged use and make mowing almost effortless. See your favorite dealer—try one today.

"Do it the easy way" booklet of "HOMKO Hints" for Home and Lawn sent on request.

ROTARY TYPE MOWERS

RIDING TYPE MOWERS

FOLD AWAY LAWN SWEEPER

For You

Western Tool
and Stamping Company, Dept. 4
2727 Second Ave., Des Moines 13, Iowa

At no obligation send me "HOMKO Hints." I enclose 10c to cover postage and mailing.

Name_____

Address_____

City_____ State_____

Western Tool and Stamping Company

The makers of Homko mowers probably figured that even devoted small-engine enthusiasts would focus on the lady of the house rather than the more mundane reel-type machine and Briggs horizontal-shaft mill, a common combo in late-1940s suburbia. My toes hurt just looking at the gal's sandals inches from Homko's spiraling blades!

Would you believe one cylinder and four carbs? This West Bend 820 by Chrysler can really move a kart, and dates from the time when Chrysler bought the West Bend Company's Hartford, Wisconsin, outboard/small-engine division.
Bob Kurkowski collection

summer of 1953, exhibited clean lines, strength, and stamina. Power-equipment manufacturers and countless consumers, often without much mechanical acumen, have enjoyed using Briggs-powered products for decades.

CHRYSLER

After Chrysler's 1965 acquisition of West Bend's outboard motor and small-engine division, the "big three" automaker thought it might be fun to dabble in the karting community. Consequently, Chrysler updated some West Bend Power Bee mills and introduced some new ones, including the 820 Series loop-scavenged two-stroke. It yielded a full 10 horsepower from 8.2 ci. Chrysler's 500 Series (a West Bend revamp) featured "cross scavenging" via a third port, pulling 4½ horses and suitable for the International Kart Federation's Rookie Stock Class. Both engines were rich with roller and needle bearings. Either would make a great find and restoration project today. By the way, the West Bend/Chrysler tradition continues with the Power Bee industrial/kart engines made by United States Motor Power. See that firm's listing for details.

Here's a nice little Canadian-built engine probably intended for washing-machine power. The 5/8-horsepower Clarke two-stroke came from the Toronto company that built the tiny Clarke Troller outboards from 1938 to 1942, as well as an air-cooled kicker in the early 1960s.

Clinton's 1950s advertising was aggressive enough to command double-page spreads in widely read magazines like the Saturday Evening Post. Here's a section of one ad plugging the small-engine line. Sometimes the company's arrowhead logo would be captioned with a mnemonic device to help people remember how to pronounce its Maquoketa, Iowa, home base. "Home of the three little Clinton injuns," it stated, "Mac, Coke, and Keeta."

CLINTON

Gazing down the assembly line of his Clinton, Michigan–based manufacturing firm in early 1945, Don Thomas wondered what he could make when World War II ended and with it his government contract for tank turret gears. The thought of returning soldiers, the new families they'd start, and all of those lawns that would need mowing around their dream homes got Thomas thinking that small engines might well be in great demand by 1946. After shifting his Clinton Machine Company to produce such motors, Thomas found he needed every one of his thousand or so employees . . . and then some. Four years later, so many Clinton engines were being sold that a bigger production facility was needed. A plant in Maquoketa, Iowa, became the company's new home, though subsequent chainsaw and outboard production occurred at the old facility. At Maquoketa during the marque's 1950s heyday,

up to 15,000 two- and four-cycle engines were being cranked out every week. Though primarily earmarked for mowers, Clinton powerplants were also used on outboard motors, garden tillers, chainsaws, small tractors, and even novelty autos like the ¾ scale 1901 Oldsmobile "replicars" of the late 1950s and early 1960s.

Clinton owns more than a footnote in karting history, too, as its A-400 Series two-strokes were enlisted by Go Kart Manufacturing Company to push some of the first commercially produced karts. The sport's seminal 1961 guide, *The Complete Book of Karting*, by Dick Day, noted that virtually every kartmaker had a Clinton option in its catalog. Later Clinton competition kart mills, like the E65-CW (clockwise crankshaft rotation) and E65-CCW (counterclockwise), had full-jeweled ball-and-needle bearings, came with kart mount brackets and sporty exhaust stacks, and were rated to run up to 6,500 rpm.

"I Coulda Been a Contender!"

In addition to the dozens of small-motor brands noted herein are arguably as many "almost" engines, usually based upon perceived competitive dynamics, that never made it to the showroom. One example is the forest-green mill on the circa-1946 Mercury lawnmower prototype. For years, Merc has been a leading maker of outboard motors, but in the late 1940s and early 1950s the fledgling company had been manufacturing significant numbers of small air-cooled engines for Disston chainsaws. Using one of its well-received single-cylinder saw motors as a basis, Mercury eyed the growing suburbanite rotary mower marketplace as a logical product-line extension. Interestingly, this two-stroke prototype (and reportedly several variations that are long gone) was deemed too expensive to produce when compared to the cheaper two-cycle Power Products and Clinton-powered rotaries being hawked by Sears and other influential retailers during the latter Truman era.

The rare Merc mower was stacked away for decades in a dark and lonely warehouse until interest in vintage outboarding drew some enthusiasts with flashlights to seek permission to investigate the premises. Among the boat motors, the mower was spotted and later lovingly restored by a Mercury history buff. He reports the engine runs nicely, but admits the machine's "cutting discs on the perimeter of a central disc" blade system left his yard looking rather chopped-up and splotchy.

Courtesy Mercury Marine

Company officials liked to boast there was "a Clinton engine for every need." During the mid-1950s, the company ran colorful full-page ads in the *Saturday Evening Post* announcing "over three million products powered with Clinton engines . . . serving homes, farms, and industry." The company had a network of 6,000 factory-authorized service centers, circa 1955, and double that by 1960. Most were tiny mom-n-pop lawnmower repair shops. No matter the franchised shop's size, Clinton urged folks to stop by in order to take advantage of a free "compression, carburetion, and ignition" checkup for any small motor. Clinton arranged its small-engine line under the following classifications:

Red Horse – Four-cycle. Heavy-duty service. Heavy-duty ball bearings on a ductile iron crankshaft. Close-grained, cast gray iron cylinder and crankcase.

Long Life – Four-cycle. Close-grained, cast gray iron cylinder and crankcase. Some versions had tapered roller bearings on the crankshaft.

GEM – Four-cycle. Lightweight diecast aluminum block with cast-iron cylinder liner and replaceable bearings. Ductile iron crankshaft.

Panther – Two-cycle. Advertised as having "only three major moving parts." Lightweight diecast aluminum block and cast-iron cylinder liner. Ductile iron crankshaft. High-performance versions (kart engines) have ball/roller bearings.

Clinton offered a host of options on its engines, such as electric starting, either as a unit that replaced the rope/rewind starter assembly or on the crankshaft under the lawnmower deck for vertical-shaft models; power take-offs; reduction gearing; and kits for converting the four-stroke engines to run on liquid propane. Clinton's 1955 publicity boasted 14 basic models (derived from the four above-noted engine classifications) and over 1,000 possible variations of these mills.

Although Clinton enjoyed the 1950s and early-1960s spotlight as "the world's most complete line" and one of the largest manufacturers of small engines, in 1964 Thomas watched Briggs & Stratton sales jump. He couldn't help but notice the Tecumseh organization edging into a greater share of his *decent quality at a low price* marketplace—especially at Sears and other large retailers that traditionally snapped up lots of lower-end Clintons for entry-level power mowers and other outdoor equipment. To remain competitive, Clinton brass needed capital for research and development, plant modernization, retooling, and product promotion. But Thomas had generously invested revenues, which some Wall Street types would have banked for a rainy day, into incentive plans and profit-sharing programs for his employees, whom he always credited for the company's success.

Greatly disappointed that no lender could be found to help him revive the firm's fiscal foundation, Thomas sold Clinton to an investment group he thought could get the company humming again. When this new ownership didn't concentrate its efforts the way Thomas and many of his old management team had hoped, numerous veteran Clinton people, who understood the company's original vision, left. The net effect of this exodus and continuing market pressures was Clinton's declaration of bankruptcy in the fall of 1966. In an effort to raise cash, some of the low-end engines sitting in factory storage were deeply discounted. Among the ready buyers was the Master Mechanic Manufacturing Company of Burlington, Wisconsin. In small *Popular Mechanics* and *Popular Science* ads, it offered a matching *pair* of Clinton A-500 two-stroke kart engines, which were normally retailed between $49 and $60 each, for $59.50!

An executive from a swimming pool filter supplier was the only interested party who offered to buy what was left of fiscally ailing Clinton. Martin Hoffinger did good things with his new 1967 venture, restarting the small-engine maker with a modest 300-person staff and some contracts with firmly entrenched outdoor equipment companies like John Deere. Through much of the 1970s, Clinton putt-putted along with small-engine and outboard-motor production. By the early 1980s, such manufacturing ceased, leaving the Clinton Engines Replacement Parts Company the sole survivor of Don Thomas' mission to build simple-to-operate, good-quality, affordable motors for every segment of the small-engine marketplace. Come to think of it, though, Thomas has many legacies—thousands of those lit-

Every small engine has a story, and if this Continental could talk, it'd tell a tale of being rescued from an abandoned garage. What makes it especially interesting is that, unbeknownst to the fellow who took the vintage single, that rickety building and associated house trailer were bulldozed by the county about an hour after he "liberated" it. Note the ignition-points box on top of the crankcase. This model represents one of the few small engines with quick access to points and condenser. Most other designs situate them under the flywheel.

tle Clintons are still humming away today on vintage pieces of equipment.

CONTINENTAL

The engines produced by Detroit-based (also Muskegon, Michigan) Continental Motors Corporation that are germane to this book include a series of circa-1950s singles ranging from 7.09- to 10.82-ci displacement. Most were of the horizontal-shaft variety and are easily recognized for their nearly horizontally slanting cylinder. Some (like the Model AU7) wore the carburetor on top of the engine, as opposed to on a manifold protruding from under the jug. Other interesting features one may find on a small Continental include a low oil-level (ignition) shutoff, mechanical three-ball governor, and ignition points conveniently housed in a little top-mounted snap-lock box. Many of the Continentals, including a less common vertical-shaft edition (with side-mounted breaker points box) needed to be rope-started.

Small-engine collectors often cite a late-1950s Continental competition model as the marque's most desirable. The competition model sports a forged connecting rod, high-lift cams, light flywheel with steel hub insert, heavy-duty 6:1 reduction gear, and a special fuel tank. Such mills brought Continental fame within the quarter-midget car racing community. Though the company hoped this success would extend to karting, its four-strokes were bested by higher-revving two-cycle competitors.

When spotting a vintage Continental, look for traces of its ornate decal. The logo features a rendering of the capitol dome in Washington, D.C., and boasts that a Continental engine is as "powerful as the nation."

CRAFTSMAN (EAGER 1)

In the late 1920s, when a Sears, Roebuck and Company executive convinced his firm to acquire the Craftsman name and brand it on a line of high-quality, brightly polished tools that he suggested Sears develop, few were confident the investment would pay off. His critics argued that people wouldn't spend money to buy good-looking hand tools, even if they came with a warranty. These skeptics' fears disappeared, however, when Craftsman wrenches, handsaws, and screwdrivers practically flew off the shelf. As consumers came to trust the marque, Sears officials extended the good name to power equipment, such as lawnmowers. Over the years, Craftsman products have been powered with engines from a number of manufacturers, most notably Tecumseh. Many of these motors were "badge engineered"—that is to say, they differ from the real manufacturers' motors in name only—so the owner of a Craftsman (or Eager 1) engine needs to do some detective work, via the ID tag and visual comparisons, to decipher the lineage.

In 1971, Sears debuted its Eager 1 mowers in a live TV commercial aired during a network sports broadcast. The ad promised that Eager 1 engines would reliably start on the first pull. The one on the TV spot, however, did not. Happily, though, in subsequent commercials, Eager 1 mills fired up with a single tug on the cord almost every time.

CUSHMAN

Long predating scooter engines from this legendary Lincoln, Nebraska, manufacturer were the two-cycle motors that cousins Clinton and Everett Cushman constructed in 1901 down in the cellar of their family home. In 1922, and in a factory setting, the Cushmans introduced their new

A 1930s Cushman Husky single. Note the long rope-start sheave pulley. It allows for either a thick or long starter cord.

Husky line of horizontal-shaft, single-cylinder, four-cycle, air-cooled engines. The Cushman logo touted, "Built light; Built right." Giving the Husky stamina were roller bearings supporting its crankshaft. Some of the Husky engines were assigned to Cushman's Bob-A-Lawn mowers, but most were purchased by folks seeking power for washing machines or some industrial/agricultural purposes.

Cushman was sold amid financial pressures during the Depression. Serendipitously, the new owner's teenage son suggested that Cushman Motor Works put its engines in motor scooters that he figured could be easily designed. The idea made Cushman a leading scooter producer for decades. Along the way, Outboard Marine Corporation owned the company, making Cushman a sister to Evinrude, Johnson, and Lawn-Boy.

EKMAN

Find one of these late-1940s, one-lung "gasoline utility" engines, and you've discovered a very rare mill that has at least two makers. That's because Ekman Engineering Company's motor was offered only in kit form, requiring the purchaser to machine its raw flywheel, crankshaft, connecting rod, piston (which was "semi-finished" at the factory), piston pin, and cowl castings. The rest of the engine's parts—such as magneto, crankcase, cylinder, carburetor, gas tank/cap, base plate, muffler, and spark plug—came ready for assembly with a "complete set of blue prints." According to a summer 1947 ad in *Science & Mechanics*, the Kansas

BUILD YOUR OWN

GASOLINE UTILITY ENGINE

1½ H.P. — 3500 RPM

Complete Parts including Set of Blue Prints $34.95

HERE'S WHAT YOU GET

Parts: Raw Casting—Flywheel, Crankshaft, Connecting Rod, Piston-semi, Piston Pin and Cowl.

Parts: Machined—Magneto, Rotor, Cylinder, Crankcase, Base Plate Cowl, Muffler, Carburetor, Tank, Line, Gas Cap, 2 Piston Rings, Spark Plug, 5 No. 6 x 3/8 Sheet Metal Screws, 2 10/32 x 3/8 Allen Cap Screws, 3 1/4-28-1-3/8 Bolts, 1 1/4-20 x 1 Bolt, 9 1/4-28 Nuts, 1 set Gasket, 2 1/4-28 x 3/4 Bolts, 11 1/4" Lock Washers, 2 Wrist Pin Rings and 1 Complete set Blue Prints.

It's easy . . . it's fun . . . to machine a few parts and assemble this powerful little gasoline motor. Blue prints show you how. Have a smooth-running, powerful engine to run lawnmower, small auto, and to furnish power for shop machines. Complete parts at amazing low price of only $34.95. Limited numbers of parts sets available. Guaranteed as represented or money back. Order yours now—send coupon with check or money order today.

ORDER DIRECT
Send Coupon NOW!

EKMAN ENGINEERING CO., BOX 186, Kansas City, Mo.

Please send me, at once, (express prepaid) complete parts (as listed) for assembling 2 H.P. Gasoline Engine. I am enclosing $34.95 (check or money order) for payment in full.

NAME ....

STREET ....

CITY .... STATE ....

For collectors of post–World War II small engines, the Ekman is about as rare as they get.

City, Missouri, manufacturer priced the potentially "smooth running, powerful little gasoline motor to run a lawnmower, small auto, and furnish power for shop machines at amazing low price of only $34.95." Nowhere did the advertisement specify whether the engine was two- or four-stroke, though one could assume it was a two-cycle job, as no valves were mentioned in the parts lineup. Also curious is the claim in the advertisement's main copy that the Ekman boasted 1½ horsepower at 3,500 rpm, while tiny print in the ad's order form pegged it at a full 2-horse rating.

EVINRUDE

This outboard motor manufacturer comes ashore here because of the ¾-horsepower air-cooled, Model 916 Speedibike engine it offered from 1932 to 1936, as well as the half-horse Model 917 Road King bicycle motor of 1934. An obscure document also shows a Model 919 Petmecky bike motor, the special three-port bicycle engine Model 935 from 1937, and the Model 949 bike motors made for Cleveland Welding Company during 1938. All were derivatives of Evinrude's two-stroke Lawn-Boy air-cooled, horizontal-shaft mower engine tagged with various model numbers (918, 928, and 929) during Lawn-Boy's initial 1932–1942 run. Mid-1930s Salsbury Motor Glide scooters used Speedibike power, carrying the Evinrude model designation Model 934. The legendary novelty mail-order house Johnson Smith and Company offered the Speedibike engine (for $59.95) in its 1935

One can only imagine where bike motors like this Evinrude Speedibike Number 916-0405 have been. Depression-era ads suggest that the 5.1-ci singles would allow operators to "run errands, ride to work, visit pals in distant towns—put 'wings' on your bicycle with this 5 to 30 mile-an-hour" engine. Though one could buy a Speedibike mill from either an Evinrude or Elto outboard dealer, the maker hoped some of its more gregarious bike motor customers would become "rider agents," signing up new buyers wherever they rode. Each Speedibike owner's manual instructed, "pull out choke button, open throttle halfway, mount bicycle, and pedal a short distance. After gaining speed, engage tire pulley. Motor should then turn over rapidly and start up after a few revolutions." Picture the little thing putt-putting to life on a sunny Friday afternoon . . . and you're off to who knows where with a refreshing breeze rushing by.

YOU'VE FOUND A NEAT OLD ENGINE . . . NOW WHAT?

It's natural to want to hear a newly acquired vintage motor purr as soon as you get it home, but patience should be your next step. Assuming that this mill's flywheel and internals turn freely, devote a few minutes to the following:

Give the unit a good external cleaning. Before doing so, be sure to cover the carburetor intake with a sandwich bag and rubber band.

Check for loose, broken, or fatally worn parts.

Remove the spark plug, ground the plug wire to the cylinder block, and while slowly rotating the flywheel or pulling the starter cord, listen or feel for any signs of rubbing, grinding, metal on metal, or abnormal friction. Be aware that sometimes the rewind starter is the primary culprit here. If suspect, it can be removed so that you can rotate the flywheel by hand. At this point, squirt a couple of shots of WD-40 penetrating lubricant or equivalent into the open spark plug hole. Some small-engine enthusiasts recommend doing so *before* beginning the "rotation/friction" test.

For a couple hundred bucks, this 1973 Simplicity looked like a good deal, but a quick manual spin of the flywheel indicated its 8-horse Briggs suffered from almost nonexistent compression.

Check for spark. Preferably a healthy zap will be immediately evident in the spark plug's gap area. If not, suspect the condenser. By the way, cleaning the spark plug is a good idea during this step.

On four-strokers, check oil level. Even if it's OK, a good policy—on an engine you'd like to run—is to get rid of the old oil and replace it with fresh lube.

For two-strokers, never yield to the temptation to run the engine without oil in the gas "for just a minute or so" to see how it runs. Once, I happened to walk by the front yard of a guy who was trying to decipher why the relatively new Lawn-Boy he'd borrowed from a neighbor had "made funny squeaking sounds and then just slowed to a stop." When the mower ran out of fuel about five minutes into the mowing job, the fellow had simply gassed it up with straight gasoline he'd had for his own machine (that was getting a tune-up in the shop) and completely cooked the Lawn-Boy. "I'm surprised how fast it seized up," he admitted after being asked if the contents of his fuel can were a gas/oil mixture.

Inspect the carburetor and air filter for signs of dirt. Clean if needed. Besides cleaning, a thorough job might include replacing the needle-valve seat and related packing, float bowl gasket, carb-to-crankcase gasket, and (if so equipped) the primer button. Also, take a look at the fuel tank cap to be sure any venting it's designed to provide is not obstructed. Old rubber fuel lines can break down inside and clog the works.

Old gas (of more than a few months) needs to go. Check fuel tank, fuel line, and strainer/filter screens for dirt and rust. Clean if needed.

Refit all previously tested parts, refuel, grasp the "struggle string," pray, and pull. When it starts, you'll have reasonable assurance that no dirt, water, debris, or loose components will be causing damage.

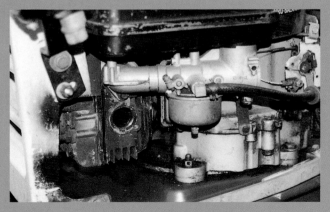

If a four-stroker has been run for a long time without a muffler, it might suffer from valve trouble.

Homelite is primarily known for two-cycle products (though in the 1960s it marketed several four-stroke outboards), so this one threw me for a loop. Upon closer inspection, it turned out to be a Briggs & Stratton vertical-shaft mill with "easy-spin" starting and a Homelite shroud. There are many instances of major motor makers branding engines for other companies to call their own.

Here's a 1930s Homelite that could light a small home, but was a pretty hefty item to tote. It's the Model D 600-watt, 110-volt generator. Check out the bronze Zenith-brand carburetor and interesting "upside down" cylinder position.

booklet, *How to Build Midget Racers and Midgetmobiles*. Also included for entry-level transportation-minded customers were "complete blueprints" detailing how one could adapt the motor to various wooden and metal homebrew vehicles.

GLADDEN
(MUSTANG MOTOR PRODUCTS)

Just a short mention here in case you happen upon a 1947–1965 Gladden-built engine originally used on its Mustang small-frame motorcycles, but sometimes adapted to other imaginative uses. Motors from the Glendale, California, manufacturer include the Series 40 and Series 50

with a 14.7-ci displacement, and the 19.4-ci Series 75. All were single-cylinder, side-valve, four-strokes in the 9½- to 10½-horsepower range. Gladden engines sometimes were referred to as the "Bumble Bee."

HOMELITE

Associated largely with quality postwar chainsaw production, Homelite is mentioned for its rugged pre–World War II single-cylinder, air-cooled engines (such as Models B and HR) for generator and pump power. Also notable are the Port Chester, New York, manufacturer's late 1950s and early 1960s saw engines adapted to kart use. Among them was the 13-pound, 1959 Model EZ-6, "a compact two-

stroke that pulled 7-hp from 5.01 cubic inches . . . featuring needle bearings throughout and a pyramid reed plate." At the height of the karting craze, Homelite followed rival McCulloch into the fray by offering complete kart and engine packages.

JACOBSEN

A leader in the late 1940s and early 1950s power-mower boom, the Jacobsen Manufacturing Company's bright-orange reel-type machines were common suburban weekend sights. The Racine, Wisconsin, firm was one of the few lawn-care equipment companies that built its own engines. Initially, most were horizontal-shaft formatted, though a move to the rotary market (via its Worthington rotary-disc mowers) was in full swing by the late 1950s. Typical of the horizontal style was a removable cylinder head, oil-bath air cleaner, outboard-supported rewind starter, and a long muffler positioned across the cylinder's underside. The head could also be removed from vertical-style Jacobsens, which were denoted by a "V" in the model designation. As two-strokes, well-running Jacobsen engines had a distinctly busy sound. Young people seeking power for homemade vehicles often eyed the horizontal incarnations. Models included the 4.71-ci J125 and J125V, 6.21-ci J175 and J175V, and a J225V yielding 7.95-ci displacement. Jacobsen horsepower range for the above-mentioned lineup ran from 2½ to 4 horses.

JOHNSON (IRON HORSE AND UTILIMOTOR)

When the Johnson outboard motor company sank into financial difficulty during the early 1930s, one of its reorganizer's plans called for the firm to diversify by manufacturing a series of small horizontal-shaft engines suitable for light utility purposes such as powering generators, mowers, pumps, and washing machines. As sister products of Johnson's Sea Horse outboards, the trade name Iron Horse seemed a likely fit. Unlike the firm's famed boat engines, though, Johnson's Iron Horse models operated on the four-cycle principle. Model series were designated in ranges X100, X200, X300 (all one-piece block/cylinder), X400, and X500 (both two-piece block/cylinder). Variations of the 5/8- to 1 1/3-horsepower singles might look like nuances to casual observers, as they included things such as different brand carburetion, customized choke activation, and drive pulleys unique to the motor's intended application. Some were fitted with kick-starters, while rope-starting and (on postwar Canadian versions) even an optional "Ready-Pull" rewind assembly were available.

Kick-starting was primarily the province of Johnson's two-stroke small-engine offering, dubbed the Utilimotor (sometimes shown as "Util-I-Motor"). The Utilimotor line

Strong as a Horse

Light as a Feather

IRON
HORSE
Model A-13

MANUFACTURED BY

RPM *Manufacturing Company*

World's Leading Manufacturer of Rotary Power Mowers
LAMAR, MISSOURI

OWNER MANUAL

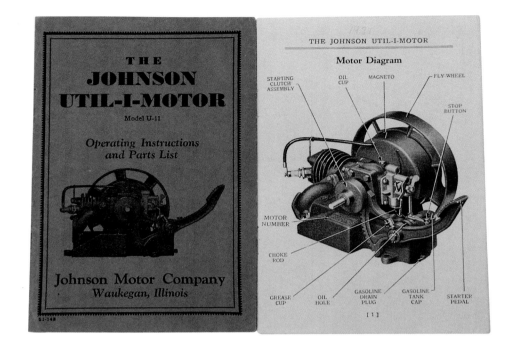

A 1931 incarnation of Johnson's two-stroke Util-I-Motor. Not only does it look like a Maytag washing machine engine, some might draw a bit of comparison to the 1940s and 1950s Jacobsen mill. Interestingly, an obscure 1937 Sears outboard service guide makes reference to certain obsolete Johnson engine parts being handled directly by Jacobsen, as if Jacobsen had bought the rights to Johnson product like the Util-I-Motor.

was Johnson's foray into washing-machine engines, which was vibrant in rural venues through the 1930s. These motors were similar to rival Maytag's engines, which also employed two-cycle operation.

After Evinrude acquired Johnson in 1936, it continued with the small-engine lines on both sides of America's northern border. Some sources indicate U.S.-made Iron Horse motors were offered from 1935 until around 1947, while Canadian production ran from 1935 through 1952. Reportedly, a short-lived two-cycle horizontal shaft–type Iron Horse incarnation was built in the Peterborough, Ontario, factory during the early 1950s. Subsequently, the Iron Horse moniker was assigned to some vertical-shaft two-stroker Evinrude/Johnson interests powering their postwar Lawn-Boy rotary mowers.

KISSEL

Admittedly a footnote listing, but the Kissel Company of Hartford, Wisconsin, merits a few lines here for a horizontal-shaft, ¾-horsepower mill it produced for Sears, Roebuck and Company from the mid- to late 1930s. The big catalog store sold a good number of the small "air-cooled, single-cylinder industrial engines" to folks who wanted to obtain power for washing machines, scooters, or saws on Sears' easy payment plan. Kissel is best known for supplying Sears with Waterwitch outboards. The little "industrial engine" was simply a slight revamp of the

smallest Waterwitch's powerhead turned sideways. West Bend Aluminum Company acquired Kissel near the close of World War II.

KOHLER

Though this engine's name appears on many kitchens and bathroom fixtures, owners of top-of-the-line garden tractors might be surprised to learn that the same Kohler, Wisconsin, firm makes both. The Kohler Company got into the engine business to diversify its plumbing base. Much of its motor output has been of the heavy-duty and even multi-cylinder variety, though typically all with a horizontal shaft.

A representative sample of Kohler engines that fit this book's single-cylinder/under-20-ci focus includes the 4-horsepower Model K91, 6¼-horse K141 and K161, and the Model K181 at 8 horsepower. Power-equipment users have long given the Kohler brand high marks for durability and stamina. Consequently, consumers are more likely to invest in a rebuild or overhaul for their trusty Kohler than they might on a nonpremium brand. It's not uncommon to find one powering an old garden tractor that's been in service for decades. Many of the now-classic International Harvester–built Cub Cadet tractors were fitted with Kohler motors. This helped introduce the marque to countless upscale suburbanites and serious hobby farmers who look for the Kohler name whenever deciding on a power-equipment purchase.

The ¾-horse cutie from Kissel was marketed through Sears in the late 1930s to those wanting economy-priced power for washing machines or other modest belt-drive applications. Wooden stands like the one that this Kissel rests on are built by engine buffs looking for a convenient way to tote and display their useful toys.

Don't drive this Bolens with bare feet unless you keep those tootsies away from the hefty rope-start sheave on that sturdy Kohler. Aside from what would today displease OSHA officials, the Bolens/Kohler combo represents rugged and long-lasting quality in garden tractors. Beautiful restoration!

LAUSON

The Lauson engine line has roots in an early-1900s 4-horse, water tank–cooled, gasoline motor that fired via a "hot tube" ignition rather than a spark plug. Neither this pioneer Lauson nor the New Holstein, Wisconsin, company's 1904 5-horse Frost King engine (cooled with calcium chlo-ride and soft water so that it could be used in below-freezing temperatures) would fit into our "small" category. Production of big motors and full-size farm tractors gave way to an emphasis on small four-cycle engine production (some as small as ½ horsepower) after the Depression necessitated a new Lauson business strategy. Typical of Lauson's

A 1930s Lauson equipped with foot starting and likely intended for washing machine drive.

Lauson's LA-815, a 1½-horse mill fitted with Timken-brand bearings. *Courtesy Tecumseh Archives*

1930s Smoothflo line of singles were the Models RA, RCM, RCR, RLC, RLM, RSC, and RSM. When the Hart-Carter Company bought the firm in 1941, it was just in time to obtain World War II contracts for building "lightweight, air-cooled engines for military applications that used aluminum alloys instead of cast iron—making them easier to transport and operate in the field." When the war ended, the makers of various machines requiring dependable powerplants snapped up Lauson engine production, among them Goodall Manufacturing Company of Warrensburg, Missouri. Its founder, Leonard Goodall (credited with inventing the rotary power mower), wanted a small-engine design that could spin his mower's blade directly off of the crankshaft. Goodall collaborated with Lauson engineers as early as 1938 to develop a vertical-shaft motor with a trio of ball bearings cushioning the crankshaft. The resulting Lauson four-stroke, vertical-crankshaft mill enlivened the pioneering Goodall rotary mowers and became widely imitated in the small-engine industry.

With an eye for expansion, the Tecumseh Products Company acquired Hart-Carter and Lauson in 1956. Lauson's small, four-cycle, air-cooled engines were then marketed under the Tecumseh Engines banner that, by 1957, included Power Products, which served as Tecumseh's two-cycle engine division. The Lauson and Power Products brands were quietly and slowly deemphasized in favor of the Tecumseh Engines moniker, which remains one of the world's leading small-engine producers.

LAWN-BOY

Famed outboard motor pioneer Ole Evinrude developed the Lawn-Boy mower in 1932. These reel-type machines typically took power from a ¾-horse, two-cycle, air-cooled engine of Evinrude design. After Evinrude's 1936 acquisition of its bankrupt competitor, Johnson outboards, the Lawn-Boy line (which had been treading water during the deepest days of the Depression) got a second lease on life with the nicely performing four-cycle Johnson Iron Horse single. Mower production ceased at the start of World War II and didn't resume until the Evinrude/Johnson concern (called Outboard Marine Corporation) eyed the burgeoning suburban homeowner as a great target market for power lawn-care equipment. In 1950, OMC officials assigned their Canadian division at Peterborough, Ontario, to come up with an especially user-friendly rotary mower for launch in the spring of 1952. Still registered to Evinrude interests, the Lawn-Boy brand name was slated to identify OMC's proposed grass cutters. During the planning process, it was learned that RPM (for *rotary power mower*) Manufacturing Company of Lamar, Missouri, had been turned over to

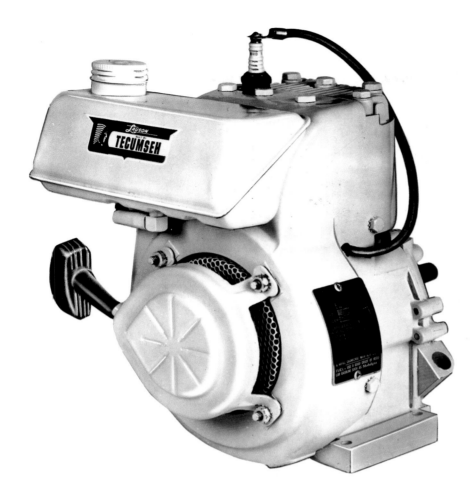

a bankruptcy receivership that was trying to sell the mower maker. Jumping into the deal the way Evinrude did with the earlier Johnson buyout, OMC picked up a respected player in the fledgling but promising rotary mower industry and secured an instant market for its newly developed (by OMC Canada) vertical-shaft Iron Horse engine. The power output of the majority of those early Iron Horse/Lawn-Boy mills earned Lamar the nickname "the two-horse town" when OMC took over operations for 1954 production.

Yielding ultimate simplicity of operation to this A Series Iron Horse mill was a governor feature incorporated into it and its two-cycle Lawn-Boy-branded successors. Unlike most any other small engine, the Iron Horse/Lawn-Boy needed no user operating adjustments other than choking, pulling the starter cord, and—after mowing—turning off (or shorting) the ignition.

The A Series engines were used beginning with Lawn-Boy's 1954 inauguration and came with bottom-end Lawn-Boy machines through 1960. Some came nonshrouded with a simple rope-start pulley, representing the most basic OMC engines. The first "sideways" (as mounted on its related mower deck) Lawn-Boy mills got a C Series designation, which continued on various Lawn-Boy models until 1971. The D motors were current from 1963 to 1982 and were some of the first Lawn-Boy engines to come equipped with "fingertip starting," a tiny pull-cord handle that could be yanked with the handle between two digits, thanks to gear reduction rewind. In 1972, the D began wearing electronic or capacitor discharge ignition. Still configured sideways, the F Series engines arrived in 1978, staying in the fray until after OMC sold the mower business to Toro at the end of the 1980s.

Each Lawn-Boy engine series has its share of enthusiasts, though C motors, and the D-400, especially when fitted with "fingertip starting," are often at the top of most two-cycle small-engine buff's favorites list. Notable Lawn-Boy products also include the completely shrouded (in a rather boxy cover) Quiet Flite introduced for 1959; the Loafer, a powered sulky that hooked to a similarly powered Lawn-Boy mower deck to create a riding lawnmower; lawn trimmers; tillers; Snow-Boy snowblowers; private-label

This 1979 Lawn-Boy 4500 has the reliable D-410 engine and fingertip starting. Years ago, I bought this for $60 from an old gentleman who included a $52.43 invoice he'd just paid the local dealership, which had installed a new air filter, fuel hose, rebuilt carburetor, and left rear wheel. Except for a $4 ignition condenser and gas/oil mixture, it hasn't cost me anything more. The lack of a "blade brake" on the handle indicates a mower is "precompliance," or produced before a 1983 law took effect mandating the blade stop whenever the operator takes his or her hands off the push grip.

Lawn-Boy machines emblazoned with the International Harvester, JC Penney, Marauder, Midland, and Lawn Cruiser identities; and the 1976 bicentennial 8234EX self-propelled walk-behind mower painted in a patriotic red, white, and blue motif. Over the years, some Lawn-Boy mowers were fitted with Briggs & Stratton and Clinton engines, and some had Packard Electric motors for customers the company predicted didn't fancy mixing up a container of oil and gas, the traditional province of Lawn-Boy owners.

The Toro people bought Lawn-Boy from OMC in 1989 and in the late 1990s introduced the remarkably environmentally friendly DuraForce two-stroke. Engines from makers like Tecumseh and Honda have also contributed to Lawn-Boy's four-cycle line.

MAYTAG

Decades prior to the postwar housing boom, Maytag washing machine motors had become household icons of dependable, portable gasoline power. Because significant numbers of rural prewar homes did not have electricity, washing machine manufacturers hoping to serve a bucolic market fitted many of their models with small engines. Though many appliance makers bought powerplants from the likes of Briggs & Stratton, Johnson, and Kissel, the Maytag people built small two-cycle engines of their own design. Often equipped with a foot pedal kick-starter, Maytag motors were available in both single-cylinder and opposed-twin formats. Air provided cooling for both versions. More than a few were converted for other purposes (such as powering rowboats, saws, mowers, pumps, and soapbox cars) when power lines finally came to the farm and the old washer got replaced with a cleaner, quieter electric version. Maytag offered "washing machine" engines (dubbed Multi Motor because of the wide application potential) from 1911 to 1952 (some say 1960s). Typically, they delivered ¾ horsepower. Most coveted by collectors is the "fruit jar" model fitted with a glass Mason jar for a fuel tank. Along the way, Maytag manufactured a lawnmower (enlivened by one of its washer motors) called the Maytag Monitor. The Iowa company's commitment to quality construction is a major reason why thousands of surviving Maytag engines can be made to run nicely today.

McCULLOCH

Combine a big inheritance with engineering skill, entrepreneurship, and a love for racing, and one can make an interesting impact on things mechanical. Robert Paxton McCulloch certainly did in the area of superchargers, quarter-midget race car engines, chainsaws, outboard motors, and karting. McCulloch's early small-engine foray included designing an opposed twin-cylinder, two-stroke car motor for the Kaiser-Frazer people, as well as building saw motors for Sears and Reed-Prentice right after World War II. From his new Los Angeles factory, he introduced a two-man chainsaw that streamlined logging. Released in 1948, the Model 5-49 (5 horsepower, 49 pounds) made most competing saws seem sluggish and weak. A similarly engineered one-man machine McCulloch put on the market shortly thereafter, further revolutionized tree-cutting and became a quick leader in the fledgling chainsaw industry. For a while, the company also moved into lawnmower production, though its most fabled rotary model used a West Bend mill. Kart historians credit the birth of karting to McCulloch's decision to withdraw from the market the mowers that unhappy owners reported falling apart, thus

Looks like this Maytag single just came out of the wash . . . a real clean machine! It's Maytag's most prolific Model 92.

No factory-built Maytag singles wore finned cylinders like this, seeing several similar versions at a gas engine show made me curious. "That's an old trick among Maytag buffs," a veteran small-engine mechanic chuckled. "Some guys mix a single's crank with an inverted twin crankcase and one of the pistons/cylinders in order to come up with a neat little hybrid."

A mean machine for vintage karting competitors is this McCulloch MC-91. The high-revving mill drinks fuel for its 6.1-ci via triple carburetors. That's a lot of intake for one cylinder! Bob Kurkowski collection

tossing the 30,000 associated West Bend engines into surplus markdown mode. In 1957, one fellow snapped up one of these West Bends, put it on a kart he'd just welded together, and ignited a nationwide obsession with the mini motorsport.

Because McCulloch chainsaw engines (all two-stroke) continued earning a great reputation for low weight and high revs, it didn't take long for someone to rig up a McCulloch Super 55A saw motor to a kart and start winning races. The kart craze came to the attention of McCulloch officials, and by 1959 the company officially got into the fray with its MC-10 kart engine, a derivative of the aforementioned saw motor. An average MC-10 would pull 5½ horses from 5.3 ci while turning 13,000 rpm. Next to be introduced was the MC-6, also 5.3 ci, but with "a racing karting carburetor with low air-flow restriction for peak performance at every angle. The piston assembly has thin rings to boost power . . . and the stroked crankshaft maintains steady power on turns and on straightaways." McCulloch skillfully engineered loop-scavenging into their mills so that, via a third port, most all of the fuel/air mixture is used efficiently to move the piston and crankshaft.

When the karting craze wound down in the late 1960s, McCulloch was still so busy cranking out chainsaws that it didn't miss a corporate beat. Many MC-10, MC-6, and other McCulloch competition kart mills were lovingly stored in a garage or basement corner because they were too good to scrap. It's not uncommon to see one auctioned on eBay today for figures that might even have surprised Bob McCulloch.

MICHIGAN MARINE MOTOR COMPANY

Around 1950, this Coldwater, Michigan, manufacturer offered a 6-horse, air-cooled four-stroke single of just under 20 ci. While primarily targeted to small boaters seeking modest inboard power, it could also be adapted to landlubber use.

MUNCIE

Better known to vintage outboard buffs than to small-engine enthusiasts, Muncie Gear Works is typically associated with its line of Neptune outboard motors that finally faded in the 1980s with a diminutive kicker called the Mighty-Mite. Even so, the Muncie, Indiana, company earns a brief mention here for a pair of landlubber engines from the 1930s: the "1-Cylinder Muncie Power Mower Utility Engine, General Utility Engine" and the "Muncie Bicycle Motor." Each featured a horizontal shaft and two-cycle operation.

Because Muncie Gear Works kept an eye on outboard motor competitor Evinrude, it took special note of Evinrude's Speedibike engine and, by 1937, had introduced a bike motor of its own. Paul Cervenka collection

O&R engines like this 1960s 1-horsepower minimill saw action on everything from bicycles to model boats. Paul Cervenka

An Onan single from the late 1930s. Most Onan engine output has primarily been designed to power electrical generators.

OHLSSON & RICE (O&R)

Begun in the 1930s as Ohlsson Miniatures, this Los Angeles–based producer of model (airplane) engines morphed into the Ohlsson & Rice Manufacturing Company, which built high-quality powerplants for modelers well into the post–World War II years. It is distinguished here from most of the hundreds of its direct model airplane motor competitors because, as O&R Engines, Inc., the firm offered tiny two-strokes (of the weed-whacker/lawn trimmer genre) to drive everything from drills and pumps to electrical generators and outboards.

ONAN

While many of this Minneapolis-headquartered manufacturer's engines are heavy-duty industrial units larger than our 20-ci cutoff (and, in some cases, multi-cylindered), the Onan brand is briefly touched upon here because its smaller motors and related electric generating plant are certainly worth acquiring and maintaining. That is to say, given the opportunity to grab one at a vintage-engine swap meet, most motorheads would jump at the chance. One to look for is the 14.9-ci, single-cylinder Series AJ. Be advised that some have battery ignition, associated generator, and an Onan-Ensign carburetor/regulator designed to burn natural gas, propane, or butane.

PINCOR (PIONEER)

Sometimes incorrectly associated with General Motors (by folks who don't pay close attention to the ID tag), Pincor engines were products of the Gen-E-Motor Corporation of Chicago. Early output from Gen-E-Motor wore the Pioneer label. For example, its 1949 Model A used the Pioneer moniker. This rope-start, horizontal-shaft, four-stroke yielded about 2½ horsepower, and with sister models AL, ALA, ALB, AM, and AG, was meant to enliven small generators, battery chargers, and lawnmowers. The Pincor engine identity might have been used to better align Gen-E-Motor to its line of power mowers bearing that name. The slogan "It's fun to pilot a Pincor!" was coined by the company's public relations people to entice postwar parents and their baby boomers to envision getting a kick out of Gen-E-Motor's lawn-care equipment. Even so, the mowers and related Pioneer/Pincor engines began fading from the landscape by the late 1950s.

POULAN

Poulan is another chainsaw producer netting a footnote here for selling some engines for kart use. About 1961, the Shreveport, Louisiana, company marketed its S-100 saw motor in either a clockwise or counterclockwise crankshaft rotation version. A major karting club set a $100 ceiling on

SAVE TIME • EFFORT • MONEY — with **MOW-MASTER** POWER MOWER

MOWS EVERYTHING

Triple Duty

1. Trims lawns velvety smooth.
2. Cuts tall weeds and grass.
3. Pulverizes leaves—abolishes raking, hauling and burning.

It's great fun to trim the lawn with the New Mow-Master. It is lighter than ever, handles like a dream and mows everything. All metal rugged construction, built for the toughest mowing jobs. Amazing New Grind-a-Leaf attachment pulverizes leaves. Surplus of smooth flowing power from improved 2 H.P. POWER-PAK Engine. See it at your dealers.

FREE booklet "POINTERS ON MAKING GOOD LAWNS" and our MOW-MASTER Literature sent upon request.

PROPULSION ENGINE CORP. Dept. SP-5
7th St. and Sunshine Rd.   Kansas City 15, Kans.

Power-Pak's 2-horse mill was touted to be so energetic that its blade could be fitted with something dubbed the "grind-a-leaf" attachment. Today we call that a "mulcher."

engines used in certain sanctioned races, so clutch and mounting brackets were optional on the $99-and-change high-revving two-stroker of approximately 5 ci, 3 horsepower, and 12 pounds. At 5.8 ci, Poulan's loop-scavenged S-200 had a slightly larger displacement.

POWER-PAK

Around 1950, Propulsion Engine Company began marketing the Mow-Master rotary power mowers. The heart of each Mow-Master was the Kansas City, Kansas, firm's 2-horse, two-cycle Power-Pak engine. An obscure engine

maker that reportedly offered product from about 1946 to 1955, the name spelling of Propulsion Engine Company's mills sometimes included a "c," making it *Power-Pack*. Machines thus labeled typically featured cowling, fuel tank, and a crankcase of sand-cast aluminum.

POWER PRODUCTS

Spunky two-strokes started rolling off Power Products' assembly line around 1946. Founders of the Grafton, Wisconsin, corporation were convinced that they could sell lots of small engines if the motors were lighter than many of the one-lung mills then on the market. According to a 1952 village profile published by the Grafton Lions Club, "initial [Power Products] production was limited to one engine model [probably the Model 1000 with cast-aluminum shrouding and a fuel tank with removable cover]." By 1952, nine models were offered. Observers believed that "through the introduction of Power Products light-weight engines, newer types of portable power equipment were being stimulated and conceived. Practically simultaneously with the introduction of Power Products engines, the rotary power mower began to grow in popularity. Manufacturers started using Power Products vertical shaft [two-cycle] engines [to the point where, by 1952, it was] the leading supplier of engines to the domestic rotary mower field, with all of the major companies (such as Sears and Montgomery Ward stores) merchandising Power Products-equipped mowers."

Beginning in the early 1950s, the firm (with some 250 employees) also delivered engines for chainsaw use. The U.S. government procurers liked the way that the company's two-strokers started in minus-40 degree Fahrenheit temperatures, and so awarded Power Products a research contract to develop small engines that would come to life at minus-65 degrees Fahrenheit. The brochure bragged that each Power Products engine was test run and "then cleaned, finished, and crated." Power Products took back used engines at its service department's "rebuilding" division. There, a customer's worn engine was rebuilt to the same specifications as a new engine "at a very reasonable cost."

In 1957 Power Products' reputation for quality small engines at a low weight and an economical price convinced Tecumseh to acquire it. Though Tecumseh couldn't have foreseen it then, the deal occurred just in time for the karting craze, providing the Power Products name another avenue in which it would gain market share success. For years, the Power Products label remained in small print (next to that of sister-product Lauson) on Tecumseh dealer signs, but eventually was completely usurped by the Tecumseh moniker.

An updated (1960s) version of the original Power Products horizontal two-stroker. Mid-to-late-1940s editions of this useful little motor featured a cast-aluminum fuel tank and shrouding, and today they make a nice addition to any small-engine collection.

Below: By the early 1950s, Power Products offered its simple and inexpensive one-lung mill in a vertical format, thus perfectly positioning the company for the Eisenhower-era deluge of rotary-lawnmower customers.

REO

Travel in a time machine to early-1950s suburbia and you'd no doubt spot a fleet of pea soup–green REO four-stroke engines helping mow many lawns there. Maybe you'd even get a glimpse of an REO single powering a small boat on the local lake. The quintessential REO cast-iron-block mill debuted in 1949, three years after its maker, truck company REO Motors (so named for Oldsmobile founder Ransom Eli Olds) of Lansing, Michigan, entered the power-mower marketplace. This introduction allowed the firm to offer its line of reel-type grass cutters with a power-plant of its own design. The nicely performing engine played a role in REO becoming the world's largest power-mower concern of 1950.

REO historian Erv Troyer notes that the company had already sold over a half-million mowers by the end of the 1951 model year, and at its peak cranked out at least 5,000 machine per week. Troyer describes REO's small motor as being "well-built, with its head slanted at 45 degrees. It ran backward—that is, the flywheel rotated counter clockwise, which was opposite from most other [small] engines . . . the power was taken from the camshaft, [resulting] in the drive pulley turning in the same direction as other engines, at half of the crankshaft speed. The intake and exhaust valves were both operated by a single lobe on the camshaft. A variation of the basic engine with a 6:1 gear reduction was used on REO's deluxe Trimalawn mower and on a REO snow blower."

Plastic-shrouded incarnations of the famed Power Products vertical engine that were successfully used in a wide variety of applications from lawn equipment to outboard motors, and served as a major reason why Tecumseh was pleased to acquire the Power Products line in 1957.

Before being morphed into a leading kart engine, the hot Power Products AH-47 (4.7 ci) was originally designed for chainsaws. Bob Kurkowski collection

When the rotary-mower boom started making significant noise around 1953, REO noticed some eroding market share and dove into the genre without first revamping its horizontal-shaft engine into a vertical-shaft format. Many vintage mower buffs consider REO's resulting Flying Cloud rotary mower one of the most visually interesting, with bulbous streamlining evocative of the early Space Age. According to Troyer, though, "rather than building an engine [for the Flying Cloud rotary] with a vertical crankshaft, [REO engineers] added a separate vertical shaft alongside the motor, driven off of the camshaft with a set of bevel gears. This shaft was connected directly to the blade on some models, while another model used a V-belt from this shaft to another jackshaft that drove the blade. There were a number of problems caused by a thrust washer that was mounted on that vertical shaft in the engine. In some, the washer would start rotating with the shaft and chew up the gear housing. [This resulted in] ground-up metal entering the crankcase," ruining the REO engine. A tiny tab on the washer would have prevented the situation. More than 5,000 of these mills had to be made good at factory expense. The firm's reputation suffered, and other mower companies pulled ahead of REO.

In 1955 and under new ownership, the REO horizontal motor was reconfigured in a vertical-shaft model by being put "on its side. The flywheel [now rotating clockwise], coil and points were moved to the opposite end of the crankshaft." This design survived through 1958, when REO's management was offered small engines from Tecumseh, badge-engineered as the REO Raider Engine, at a cheaper unit price than REO spent to manufacture its own motors.

Sure cure for Spring Fever

REO ROYALE DE LUXE POWER MOWER

WIDER 21" CUT;
BIGGER 1¾ hp.
4-cycle REO
ENGINE

REO was just one of many mower makers that suggested firing up its small engine and doing the lawn represented more fun than the circus, baseball, or even romance (according to another colorful ad in which a young man operating his REO ignored a waiting convertible filled with beautiful girls). Because reel-type mowers like this were self-propelled, more than a few were used to tow wagons. The result was a primitive "riding mower" or "motor vehicle" on which some adventurous youngsters took trips far from the backyard. Speaking from experience, I can say that the pavement did little to keep tread on those hard rubber tires, and any sand, debris, or dust hit by the spiraling blades could make the driver's face sting. By the way, the pictured REO mill yielded 1¾ horsepower and had the brand's telltale red rubber starter grip and oil fill nut, and an unpainted louvered sheetmetal air-cleaner cover. With its mower unit, this one retailed for $136.95 in 1952.

Tecumseh's first engines were rebadged Lauson four-strokes, like this inertia-start model.

SALSBURY MOTOR DIVISION

A slant-head four-stroker, the Salsbury Model 600 air-cooled single generated 6 to 6½ horsepower. The early-1950s 19.4-ci mill came from Pomona, California.

SIMPLEX (SERVI-CYCLE)

A few lines are appropriate for this small motorcycle engine, because some were liberated from their host's frame and given a new life doing other things. Produced from 1936 into the 1960s, the New Orleans–built Simplex (also known as Servi-Cycle) motors came in a 7-ci displacement, as well as a postwar version of 8 ci. The piston-ported two-strokes wore a very short crankshaft that only ran in one bearing (near the flywheel), thus requiring no support on the other side.

TECUMSEH

Engines wearing the Tecumseh banner were originally off-shoots of its four-stroke Lauson and two-cycle Power Products divisions, acquired in 1956 and 1957, respectively. Founded in 1930 by Ray Herrick, whose workers affectionately dubbed him "the Ol' Man," Tecumseh began life

Compare the early twenty-first-century Tecumseh two-stroker with the rope-start Power Products from the 1950s. While the Formula 3.0 is much more environmentally friendly, and has an automatic compression release for nearly effortless starting, a fuel gauge, and a convenient fuel-priming bulb, one can see the obvious lineage of Power Products' basic but sound design.

CAN I STILL GET PARTS FOR THAT?

Small engines are small, so it makes sense to believe that their parts are even smaller. That being the case, one can safely assume tons of parts—for both current and long-obsolete motors—are waiting to be discovered everywhere from store shelves to cigar boxes at garage sales. Another encouraging amateur mechanic's truth worth embracing is the fact that parts that you don't absolutely need now will usually be a lot cheaper if you can wait. That's because engine enthusiasts who enjoy spending time talking to fellow motorheads, hitting the engine-related meets and flea markets, searching through lawnmower graveyards, checking in with the power-equipment repair shop, and connecting with other buffs on small-engine websites are likely to find needed parts and literature—and probably a few interesting items they didn't know they needed. Don't forget to try the small-engine department (even if it comprises only a single pegboard with generic tune-up kits) at your local auto parts franchise. Online venues where you can get specific engine model/year information, ask basic questions, and maybe download a service booklet for free are as dynamic as the Internet itself. Fortunately, this means that whenever one mysteriously disappears,

Unless you're willing to miss some buried treasure, never dismiss a small-engine graveyard as "just a pile of junk." It's a good policy, though, to wear work gloves and old clothing when pawing through such motor mountains.

another soon materializes to continue the enthusiasts-helping-enthusiasts tradition. (Always try finding the latest offering about your engine of interest via a web search.) These sites are great places to start your parts quest, especially when you try their various links. As of publication time, some of my favorites included:

www.asecc.com — The Antique Small Engine Collector Club's official site
www.classic-engines.com — A good small-engine reference web address
www.rearenginekarts.com — Kart power of the 1950s and up
www.vintagekarts.com — Another very interesting early-era karting/kart-engine locale
www.ruppbikes.com — Minibike information from days gone by
www.simpletractors.com — Classic Simplicity garden tractor buffs run this one
www.acresinternet.com/cscc.nsf — Detailed site for vintage chainsaw collectors

A 1970s Tecumseh with Lauson lines, Ezee-Start rewinder, and carburetor shrouding set the stage for the company's well-received foray into the snowblower engine marketplace, via its Snow King series.

as the Hillsdale (Michigan) Machine Tool & Tool Company. The Tecumseh moniker was adopted four years later, when Herrick moved his firm to Tecumseh, Michigan. Soon, the company shifted its emphasis from making a variety of small auto parts, tools, and pieces for refrigerators, to concentrating on producing refrigeration compressors. In 1939, Tecumseh's output hit 160,000 units a year. During the war, the firm made shell casings but jumped right back into the compressor business when the fighting ended. Consumer demand for new refrigerators and the recently introduced room air conditioners gave Tecumseh abundant outlets for its compressor line. Herrick plowed profits into expansion, and entering the small-engine industry seemed like a natural extension. Describing the 1950s acquisition of Lauson and Power Products, a Tecumseh publicity brochure aptly states, "the addition of these two made Tecumseh a leader in the outdoor power-equipment industry virtually overnight."

For several years, the Power Products (the two-stroke line) and Lauson (four-cycle) names were prominently featured, but by the mid-1960s were reduced to small-print identities sandwiched between Tecumseh Engines text boxes under the parent company's Indian chief logo. The

stately image, in the form of sheetmetal signs and lighted advertising clocks, quickly became a central theme at literally thousands of small-engine establishments, from well-heeled suburban outdoor equipment centers to one-man lawnmower fix-it shops headquartered in lopsided backyard sheds.

Tecumseh's engine résumé is so large that only a random representation fits in this section. (Thousands of units from the 1969 line can still be found in service, or, possibly, looking for a good home.) In the Power Products two-cycle tradition, Tecumseh offered four singles displacing 5.1 ci and creating 2½ horsepower:

Vertical-shaft T633 (rewind) and T637 (rope start) designed for rotary mowers.

Vertical-shaft T634 "designed and engineered exclusively for outboard motors (such as the entry-level Commando and Lancaster Guppy), and featuring full outboard (spark and throttle advance/retard) controls." This one could be had in a 3½-horse version, too.

Horizontal-shaft T1376 built for "general industrial applications and reel-type mowers." Though wearing a sheetmetal fuel tank, the T1376 was an offspring of one of the original Power Products' best-loved engines, a rugged

The contemporary Tecumseh two-cycle Snow King for smaller snow-removal applications is sometimes commandeered by karters.

little horizontal-shaft mill with a cast-aluminum tank and shrouding.

Models AH47, AH58, and AH81 were high-rpm engines Tecumseh made for chainsaw manufacturers. Some made their way onto the kart track.

Lauson lineage was represented in these vertical four-strokers:

LAV30. Lawn and garden applications in 2½-, 3-, and 3½-horsepower versions and 7.75 ci.

LAV35. For lawn and garden equipment in 2½-, 3-, and 3½-horsepower versions and 9.06 ci. Another LAV35 with a small, rear-attached gas tank (as opposed to an integral tank positioned under the rewind starter) was built for lawn tiller and industrial uses.

Tecumseh's overhead-valve Enduro XL (6 1/2 horsepower) is considered a versatile utility engine and has seen action in industry, consumer power equipment, minibikes, and karts.

V40 in 4-, 5-, and 6-horsepower versions and 11.06 ci. Made for small riding lawn and garden equipment.

V50 in 4-, 5-, and 6-horsepower versions and 12.2 ci. For medium-size lawn and garden or industrial applications.

V60 in 4-, 5-, and 6-horsepower options. This 13.5-ci engine came without a fuel tank for use in "highly styled lawn and garden riding applications" where the mower maker incorporates its own fuel reservoir under the lawn/garden tractor's hood or cowl.

Horizontal-shaft Tecumseh four-strokes in the Lauson tradition, circa 1969, include:

H22. 7.35 ci in 2-, 2½-, 3-, and 3½-horsepower ranges. "Quiet, smooth, relaxed power for light applications, especially reel-type lawnmowers."

H30. 7.75 ci in the same horsepower ranges as the H22, but dubbed "heavy duty for agricultural tiller and industrial applications."

H50. This is an early Snow King engine for which Tecumseh is so well known in the snowblower marketplace. Available in 4-, 5-, and 6-horsepower styles, the

12.2-ci mill was specifically "designed for snow removal equipment and cold weather applications . . . NOT a winterized summer engine." In addition to the aluminum-block model, it was offered in cast iron.

H60 (and HH60 with cast-iron cylinder block). 4-, 5-, and 6-horsepower from 13.55-ci displacement. Best for garden tractors and industrial use.

HH80. 8- and 10-horsepower versions available in rope-start format. Cast-iron cylinder block. 19.4 ci. At 85 pounds, this one was most suited for "heavy duty service on small commercial and agricultural tractors."

Other Tecumsehs difficult for small-engine buffs to pass up include circa-1983 models HS40 (4 horsepower) and HS50 (5 horsepower) with a 20-degree slant from their engine mounts. These four-strokers with long-neck muffler pipes were specifically designed for minibike applications. The Model AH520, a 2-horse, two-cycle Snow King engine (also in 2½ horsepower) is interesting because the snowblower genre is typically four-stroke-oriented, with at least a 5-horse output. Another neat Tecumseh to watch for is the company's early twenty-first-century OHH65 Fun

A favorite in the modern kart community is Tecumseh's Power Sport high-performance 11-horse four-stroker, fitted with overhead valves.

Power 6½-horse kart engine, as well as the company's 5-horsepower Star "motor sports" racing mill.

The Tecumseh small-engine line is one of the industry's most robust. It is likely that any small-engine enthusiast who enjoys collecting, revitalizing, and running "vintage" (a title that expands with each passing year) Tecumseh-branded motors will never be bored with his or her hobby.

TORO

Long before Minneapolis-based Toro fitted its line of lawnmowers and other outdoor products with motors from major makers like Briggs & Stratton, it produced small engines. Typical of this pre–World War II output was Toro's 3½-horsepower Model MF, a four-stroke single with horizontal shaft.

The Toro-built M.F.

UNITED STATES MOTOR POWER

Since 1991, this East Troy, Wisconsin, manufacturer has served as successor to the West Bend/Chrysler small-engine line. It picked up the rights to the lineage's design from the Mercury outboard organization that had acquired it—primarily for the Force (formerly Chrysler) Outboard inventory and tooling—in the 1980s. United States Motor Power offers contemporary versions of the famed West Bend/Chrysler 580, 700, and 820 Series Power Bee engines.

UNITED STATES MOTORS CORPORATION

Produced around 1950 in 1¾-, 2¼-, and 4½-horsepower versions, air-cooled singles from this firm's Oshkosh, Wisconsin, factory had a marine focus, though some saw action in land-based venues.

WEST BEND

It may seem curious that one of the world's biggest small-appliance manufacturers is connected to small-engine history, but the West Bend Company certainly has a past rich in two-stroke heritage. The West Bend, Wisconsin, firm's motor story begins around 1944, when it bought the Kissel outboard motor plant. After the war, West Bend's new Hartford, Wisconsin, engine facility produced outboards for Sears under the Elgin name and established a good reputation for designing and building two-stroke boat motors. One of the first was an air-cooled, 1¼-horse kicker that served as a basis for its West Bend Series 2700 engines, which were meant for mowers and other land-based uses. Cubic inch displacement within this line ranged from 3.76 to 5.10.

A quick check of the McCulloch listing notes how, around 1956, one of a slightly later run of West Bends, supplied to McCulloch to power its rotary mowers, became a catalyst for karting. West Bend took serious notice and started designing engines specifically for the karting crowd. In 1960, the company built an asphalt kart track next to its factory. The "track combined a 1/10th mile oval and 2/10th mile road course" and was constructed to better facilitate research and development in high-revving two-cycle mills with race-winning pedigrees. The West Bend 500 Series, Model #580 (5.8 ci) sprang from this R&D to see many a checkered flag.

Other notable West Bend powerplants from the Kennedy era include the 510, 645, and 700. Any aftermarket hop-up shop worth its salt supplied high-perform-

ance accessories like a tuned exhaust stack and dual-carb manifold for West Bend engines. The engine marque went the way of the wind when West Bend sold its outboard and small-motor division to Chrysler around 1965 (see United States Motor Power listing).

WHIZZER

Their nostalgic connection with youthful, Truman-era basic transportation has driven the price of vintage Whizzer bicycle motors through the roof. From 1939 through the mid-1950s, several incarnations of a four-stroke single mainly intended for installation on a bike made the Whizzer name synonymous with low-price, two-wheeled motoring. The Pontiac, Michigan, company had secured the rights to the Whizzer from a modest California manufacturer.

The biggest sellers of the Whizzer line were its Model J (1948–1949) and 300 Series (1949–1952). The company went into other product areas around 1955, but continued offering Whizzer parts for a decade. Reportedly, the remaining inventory, including 175 motors and some official Whizzer motorbikes, was picked up in 1970 for about $5,000 by an engine buff who then sold them at antique-car swap meets. Before whizzing to the next brand, it should be noted that revival versions of Whizzer motors have been introduced over the years, including a two-stroke, .95-horsepower imposter from around 1976. Be sure you know what to look for when seeking a genuine "original" example.

Now here's a small engine that looks heavy-duty, even when sitting in a farm field. This powerful Wisconsin single, with its cast-iron block, is a bear to lift, but says "bull" to anyone doubting it can handle substantial loads. Note how many bolts hold the thing together. Many old-timers suggest the higher the engine's quality, the further its component assemblies can be taken apart for internal inspection and servicing.

57

When the designers of the David Bradley Tri-Trac required rugged power for their small-farm tractors, they equipped this 1954–1957 version with a 6-horse Wisconsin mill.

WISCONSIN (ROBIN)

Products of the Wisconsin Motor Corporation are tagged "Heavy-Duty Air-Cooled Engine," identifying the Milwaukee manufacturer's products as being designed for industrial use. Single-cylinder versions appropriate for our study are the 10.9-ci Model AA; the 6-horsepower, 14.9-ci Model ALN; and the 7-horse Model BKN, displacing 17.8 ci. Devotees of high-end garden tractors often associate the Wisconsin brand with long-lasting and reliable power.

Some of Wisconsin's smallest motors wear the Robin label and are represented by the EY18W, an 11.14-ci engine yielding 4.6 horsepower, the EY25W at 6.5 horsepower and

IS THAT ALL OF THEM?

Most every community has at least one eccentric resident who takes delight in creating a personal junkyard spilling from some ramshackle outbuilding. Typically, its metal mounds include lots of scattered small engines and related lawn and garden equipment. While most of that stuff's sun-faded and scratched nameplates are represented in this historical listing, there's a chance a few have come from minor motor makers that eluded this catalog. But that's what

makes the small-engine hobby fun—one never knows when a mechanical mystery will appear.

As a matter of fact, references to several additional makers popped up shortly before publication. These include 1930s air-cooled four-strokers from Nelson Brothers of Saginaw, Michigan; the 1-horse, two-cycle Diamond Junior (a.k.a. the Dodd and the Hume), circa 1909, via the Diamond Engine Company of Des Moines; and two-stroke Redemotor washing-machine engines out of the Elgin (Illinois) Wheel & Engine Company from 1911 to the 1920s.

If you've come across a brand that should be added to a subsequent edition of *The Small-Engine Handbook*, feel free to contact me via MBI Publishing Company, or a web search of my name. Meanwhile, keep looking through any junkyard, yard sale, or farm auction that seems interesting—the next one might contain a single-cylinder gem waiting to be adopted. Each one has the potential to make you an even more knowledgeable small-engine buff and provide you with a working piece of history.

Available separately or ready-to-ride on a factory-built motorbike like the Pacemaker with front suspension, Whizzers were on the wish lists of many a young would-be motorist during the 1940s and 1950s.

SHORT PROFILES OF MANUFACTURERS

CHAPTER 3
OPERATION AND TROUBLESHOOTING

Logic may say otherwise, but anyone who has even a single season's worth of experience running a one-lung, air-cooled motor knows the little engine possesses a definite personality. Some are like a faithful dog, never failing to come when called—or to start when cranked. Others might be reminiscent of an undependable coworker who sputters lots of promises but never ends up doing much. And more than a few could be compared to that fickle someone who seems fine for a while and then, for no apparent reason, decides to quit or refuses to restart the relationship despite having just expressed tremendous satisfaction.

Like pooches and people, every small engine, though manufactured in the commonality of an assembly line, is a unique product of its lineage, birth, upbringing, and subsequent treatment. Of course, there are examples of seriously rusty, poorly maintained single-cylinder engines having lived outdoors under a tattered tarp for a decade that are still willing to fire up with only several pulls on the duct-taped starter cord. Perhaps these are among the fabled "runs like a top" legion that industrial efficiency experts say were probably assembled on a Tuesday, when workers are most attentive, and are of a proven design with components that fit perfectly. Truth is, though, no carelessly treated small engine will perform well for long, but with a few exceptions every motor has the potential to display the personality of a trusted friend. It's mostly a matter of knowing what your small engine is all about, as well as how to help it stay friendly and happy.

In describing small engines and their idiosyncrasies, we'll identify them as having either a *horizontal shaft* (crankshaft) or a *vertical shaft*. The horizontal shaft is good for powering minibikes, karts, pumps, generators, garden tractors, and old-fashioned reel-type mowers. The vertical-shaft format was made popular by rotary mowers.

Rope start, in which a cord is wrapped around a sheave pulley on the end of the crankshaft, is the most basic version of either style, although the rope start is virtually

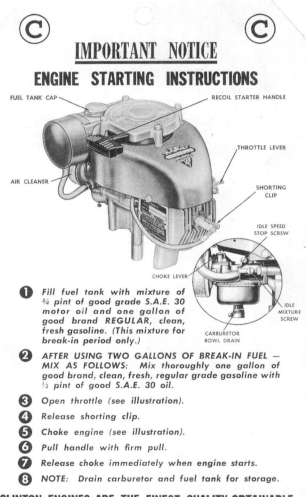

IMPORTANT NOTICE
ENGINE STARTING INSTRUCTIONS

FUEL TANK CAP — RECOIL STARTER HANDLE — THROTTLE LEVER — SHORTING CLIP — IDLE SPEED STOP SCREW — CHOKE LEVER — IDLE MIXTURE SCREW — CARBURETOR BOWL DRAIN — AIR CLEANER

1. Fill fuel tank with mixture of ¾ pint of good grade S.A.E. 30 motor oil and one gallon of good brand REGULAR, clean, fresh gasoline. (This mixture for break-in period only.)
2. AFTER USING TWO GALLONS OF BREAK-IN FUEL — MIX AS FOLLOWS: Mix thoroughly one gallon of good brand, clean, fresh, regular grade gasoline with ½ pint of good S.A.E. 30 oil.
3. Open throttle (see illustration).
4. Release shorting clip.
5. Choke engine (see illustration).
6. Pull handle with firm pull.
7. Release choke immediately when engine starts.
8. NOTE: Drain carburetor and fuel tank for storage.

CLINTON ENGINES ARE THE FINEST QUALITY OBTAINABLE. CARE AND CONSIDERATION WILL ASSURE EXTRA LONG LIFE

Treat a small engine right as soon as you get it, and that little mill will loyally reward you with motor music from the first pull of the starter cord. It's wise to heed introductory instruction tags, but every once in a while there's an engine that just doesn't seem to like the idea of all that work—no matter what you do.

extinct in the new-engine marketplace. Also extinct are the crank-up "inertia" starters of the 1960s. Both types have long since been replaced with *rewind* (recoil) *starting*, and, in some cases (especially for snowblowers), electric starting.

No cranking of any kind is possible if a motor is *stuck*, *seized up*, or *set up*, all synonyms for the piston being fused to the cylinder walls due to rust, overheating, or lack of lubrication. On any engine you're considering, rotate the flywheel (or pull the starter cord) to, in turn, rotate the crankshaft and move the piston within the cylinder. It should *turn over* easily or, in the vernacular, be *free*. Speaking

"How come you're selling this one?" I asked a vintage-engine meet exhibitor who had about 10 other small motors displayed next to his camper. "Because he can't get the darn thing to run!" his wife laughed from a lawn chair. Even so, I figured that the rope-start, horizontal-shaft Briggs with oil-bath air filter was a bargain—until I spent a whole Saturday trying this and that and frequently pulling on the cord. Today, though, its subsequent owner tells me "she purrs like a contented kitten" since he noticed that what I thought was the timing mark (on the crankshaft-mounted gear) was actually a scratch from a careless screwdriver. When the real timing mark was deciphered (under a bit of grime) and lined up with one on the camshaft, this story enjoyed a happy ending.

of synonyms, *jug* is an old term for a mill's cylinder, and some call a *camshaft* the *bump stick*. Additionally, *stroke* and *cycle* (whether two or four) can also be used interchangeably.

Key components of an engine of any size include a *crankcase*, in which the *crankshaft*, *connecting rod* (hinged to the piston via the piston pin or wrist pin), and *end cap* or *rod cap* move. The crankcase of a four-cycle motor gets partially filled with oil so that the moving parts can be lubricated. Typically, oil is splashed into places it's needed by way of a paddle "dipper" affixed to the end cap, from the rotation of a scatter wheel typically meshed to the camshaft, or via a pump geared to the crankshaft or camshaft. In two-cycle engines, oil is mixed with gasoline and gets distributed by the associated fuel flow through the crankcase and cylinder, onto the piston, and into the bearings.

While some small engines are designed with a *cylinder block* that's detachable from the crankcase, many crankcase castings are produced in one piece (or "en banc") to include the cylinder block. The *cylinder head* is characteristically removable in a four-stroke to provide access to the *fuel intake* and *exhaust valves*. These valves are pushed up via a tappet bumped by cams on a camshaft driven off a gear meshed to a mate gear on the crankshaft. Two-strokers (with rare exceptions like 1946–1954 Martin outboard motors) don't use mechanical valves. Consequently, the cylinder head may or may not come off, though one that detaches is often preferred by those wanting to check the piston crown or perhaps increase compression by "milling" the head (shaving down the surface where the head mates to the cylinder) to increase compression.

The *piston*, with its associated *piston rings* providing a tight seal, travels up and down in the cylinder, and in so doing, rotates the crankshaft. A *flywheel* is typically keyed onto the crankshaft. Weight from the flywheel provides rotational momentum. Most small engines are *magneto*-fired. Magnets for establishing an electrical field usually reside in the flywheel's perimeter and pass by the metal heels of a coil, which (along with a condenser) help provide power to make the spark plug spark. "Make or break" *ignition points* (or, an electronic ignition module that takes the place of traditional points) act as a switch that turns on power to the plug at just the right time for it to ignite the fuel/air mixture in the top of the cylinder, thus shooting the piston down the cylinder. When this happens, the motion causes friction and heat. Fins on the cylinder block and head exterior act to dissipate the heat. Fan blades cast into the whirling flywheel also aid in the "air-cooling" process. On some small engines, the stiff breeze from the flywheel fan at full operating speed (or maximum desired crankshaft rpm) moves a rudder vane that in turn activates a rod linked

A camshaft gear meshed to the crankshaft gear. Timing marks on each show proper placement. Those cams (or bumps) on the camshaft help move the valves. This is four-stroke equipment.

to the carburetor throttle. This motion is set to stop at a manufacturer-specified point, keeping the engine's speed at a safe rpm for its design. Because the function serves to regulate, its assembly is dubbed a *governor*. Some governors, like those in many Lawn-Boy mills, are activated by springs and centrifugal force.

Bearings are used to greatly reduce friction at critical contact locations, such as where the crankshaft runs through the crankcase. Bearings may be of the plain bronze bushing style or have the "frictionless" characteristics of a ball, roller, or needle bearing. The higher the engine's quality, the greater likelihood it will be equipped with frictionless bearings wherever possible. Bearings that support a part (such as a crankshaft) that protrudes through the crankcase not only need to provide a smooth ride, but must also keep crankcase pressure, fuel/air mixture, and oil from leaking out. *Seals*, often made of rubber or plastic, are used for this vital purpose.

Traditionally, every small engine sips *fuel* from a *tank* (often via gravity feed) and converts it into fuel/air vapor by venturi action in its *carburetor* (sometimes called a "carb"). Compression within the crankcase draws in the fuel vapor and moves it toward the cylinder head, where it is further compressed between the head and piston crown. In two-strokes, *reed valves* (thin little metal gates in back of the carb that let in the proper amount of fuel vapor, but block entry at appropriate timing intervals) or a *rotary valve* (as simple as a pie-shape cut in the crankshaft that's capable of scooping

The piston and its connecting rod and end cap (or rod cap) secured to the crankshaft. The big "oil control ring" (third piston ring from the top) indicates this came from a four-cycle engine. Unlike conventional compression rings, the oil control ring is supposed to wipe the oil from the cylinder walls back into the crankcase. Should oil get past this ring and into the combustion chamber, plug fouling, oil burning, and poor performance will result.

Timing marks properly aligned. It sure makes a difference when they are!

Close inspection reveals a cam activating a valve tappet that in turn lifts the (unseen) valve.

up the misty fuel mix) wing the vapor to the top of the piston and cylinder through *intake cylinder ports*. Spent fuel (or exhaust gases) exits the cylinder via exhaust ports, also positioned in the cylinder wall, and on to the *muffler*. Four-cycle mills direct exhaust to their muffler by way of the previously mentioned cam-activated exhaust valve.

Finally, many manufacturers cover at least part of their small engines with *shrouds* or *cowling*. At first, companies did this simply to make their motor look a bit streamlined and provide it with a smooth surface for a brand logo or identification plate. As consumers, government, and industry became more safety conscious, shrouding was seen as a necessary way to keep hands out of spinning flywheels, rope-starter sheaves, and hot parts. Like the province of many components that were redesigned to be lighter and cheaper to produce, cowling has gone from steel to aluminum to

"HEY, HAND ME THAT WRENCH"

While few veteran small-engine enthusiasts advocate using the edge of a dime for a screwdriver, most will suggest that novice mechanics can do wonders with a simple set of tools. To get started, assemble the following. In fact, it's quite probable that many of its members are already at hand.

Screwdrivers — Small, medium, and large in standard slot, as well as Phillips-head formats

Adjustable Wrench — The 8-inch denomination is a good all-around size and could become your favorite item on the tool board

Feeler Gauge — For checking spark plug gaps, valve clearances, and piston ring play

Spark Tester — Can be homebrew (see page 15)

Small Hammer — For tapping (never banging) on stubborn parts

Block of Oak — For softening the hammer's blow

Small Flat Metal File (and/or sandpaper) — To lightly dress ignition points and other small parts that require de-burring or smoothing

¼- or ⅜-Inch Socket Wrenches — In sizes from ³⁄₁₆ to ½ inch, plus a deep ¹³⁄₁₆-inch socket for spark plug work

Open End/Box Wrenches — From ⅜ to ¾ inch

Pliers — Standard, locking, and needle-nose

Allen Wrenches — A basic set

Pump Squirt Oil Can — Filled with fresh lube

Once you feel like increasing your shop's tool inventory, you can add items like a wider range of wrench sizes, nut drivers, a small pipe wrench, offset screwdrivers, drive punch pins, tap and die set, chisel, wire stripper, flywheel puller, hacksaw, bench grinder fitted with a wire wheel, air compressor, magneto/coil tester, cylinder hone, piston-ring compressor, drill press with bits, bearing (reamer) removal/installation tools, and propane torch. Commercially available compression testers and the Ignition Chek, an ingenious and affordable device that allows for detecting magneto problems that exist under cylinder compression, are both useful additions to any small-engine shop.

A great way to economically augment your toolbox is to cruise garage sales for quality vintage American-made tools. I've picked up some classics in the 50-cent to five-dollar range and find that they almost always clean up nicely and feel solid on the job.

A feeler gauge is used to measure spark plug gap. Be sure the engine is fitted with its recommended plugs per spark plug manufacturers' charts at point-of-purchase store displays. For older models no longer noted on contemporary guides, consult vintage-engine Internet sites (or the more detailed store-based plugs listings) that offer the latest spark plug makers' conversion charts to match obsolete plug numbers with current versions.

Measuring valve stem–to–tappet (or valve lifter) clearance with a long feeler gauge. Correct clearances allow the valve to seat completely, as opposed to staying open at times it is designed to be closed.

Throw in a feeler gauge, and this basic collection of hand tools will go a long way in helping to diagnose and repair small engines. That 8-inch adjustable wrench was a freebie tossed out by someone who couldn't budge its rusty jaws. A bit of penetrating oil, tapping, and cleanup on a wire wheel soon made it one of the most useful tools in the set. Most of the screwdrivers came from a lawn sale that had a cardboard carton marked, "anything in this box 50 cents."

After removing the cylinder head and looking down at the valves, it is evident one is for fuel/air intake (IN) and the other serves to exhaust (EX) spent gases. If they don't properly seat and open, engine performance either suffers or doesn't happen.

Sure, most mechanics might use their hands to remove or install piston rings, but this handy "piston ringer" (above and below) from the 1930s can save fingernails as well as brittle piston rings.

plastic. Though it does not improve performance, metal shrouding with the engine maker's name indelibly cast into it is the widespread favorite type among most classic-motor enthusiasts. It gives a buff reason to smile, "Ah, they sure don't build 'em like that anymore!"

TWO-CYCLE (OR TWO-STROKE) OPERATION

This longest-produced type of engine gets its name from delivering power via performing those five events outlined in the sidebar on page 68. The motor is designed with intake ports to introduce fuel/air mixture to the cylinder, and exhaust ports to allow spent gases to exit the cylinder and make room for the next "charge" of mixture to be ignited by the spark plug. Stroke one, accomplishing *intake* and *compression*, gets under way as the crankshaft rotates and moves the piston up the cylinder. The fuel/air mixture previously sucked into the crankcase (by crankcase pressure) and introduced through the intake porting in the cylinder wall, is compressed in the uppermost area of the cylinder. At this point, the piston covers or blocks off the intake and exhaust ports. Stroke two includes *power* and *exhaust*. With an easily combustible fuel/air mixture in the tightly compacted area between the piston crown and cylinder head, and right under the spark plug, "fire" from the spark plug, timed to go when the piston reaches an optimum point at or near top dead center (TDC), ignites the mixture. The

Here, the exhaust valve is open, which—with the cylinder head present—would let burned gases escape to the muffler and beyond.

With valves removed, paper arrows represent fuel intake and exhaust routing.

Looking through the crankcase breather area, we can see valve stems and the springs that keep them closed until they are bumped up by the cam. A "keeper" holds the spring in place by sliding into a groove (or being held by a pin) in the valve stem. Note, through the carburetor manifold, the top of the valve stem.

resulting explosion shoots the piston back down the cylinder, rotating the crankshaft. As the piston descends, fresh fuel/air mixture waiting in the crankcase gets squished to the point where it's looking to go up to the cylinder via the intake ports as soon as the piston uncovers that pathway. These passages open slightly after the exhaust ports have been uncovered so that the hot, highly pressurized exhaust gets a head start out of the engine. The rush of burned fuel/air mixture out of the cylinder (and outside through the muffler) makes way for the fresh fuel/air charge to blow through the intake porting and (as soon as the piston blocks off the ports) get compressed in the cylinder. There, it's ready for an ignition spark that begins the two cycles again.

TWO-STROKE LUBRICATION

Late-nineteenth and early-twentieth-century incarnations of the two-stroke engine took straight gasoline in their fuel tanks and lubrication in "drip oilers" typically piped directly to the bearings and cylinder walls. In fact, some manufacturers decreed that any other way of doing things would void the motor's warranty. Some speculate the first person to add a bit of oil in his two-stroker's gas tank did so not because of mechanical genius, but out of sheer laziness. Whatever the motivation, word quickly spread that mixing oil and gas in a two-cycle engine's fuel tank worked fine and was a great idea, because it ensured a supply of lube to crankcase and cylinder, plus all associated moving parts, whenever the motor was running. Over the years, engine manufacturers' recommendations on specific gasoline/oil

SETTING UP A SMALL-ENGINE SHOP LIKE A PRO

When an early-1950s issue of *Implement & Tractor* suggested its readership might benefit from a boom in hobby farm and garden power-equipment sales, the magazine partnered with Jacobsen Manufacturing Company to plan the ideal small-engine service shop. Some of the dream facility's features—like the manager's office, parts department, display counter, and passé bed-knife grinder and mower grinder for reel-type mowers—are extravagant by hobbyists' standards. Even so, the layout, with its purpose-dedicated work stations, sets the stage for conducting repairs or full restorations without the bench-top clutter and confusion that often leads to misplaced parts and general chaos that tends to grow during any project. In any shop setup, clutter-free space—and lots of it—is key. Admittedly, though, abundant square footage is a luxury many of us don't have.

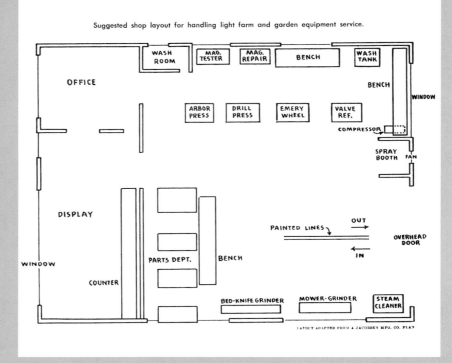

This diagram for a suggested small-engine shop layout appeared in an early-1950s magazine.

That being the case, if the schematic prompts the addition of even one more small tabletop area for conducting a specific task (such as magneto testing and revitalization), it will aid in your small-engine endeavors.

Two of three workbenches in the author's basement shop. Because the horizontal surface closest to any entrance usually gets quickly cluttered, it's always a battle to keep bench tops free of stuff unrelated to the project at hand. By the way, the white pegboard makes the tools stand out for convenient selection. Replacing tools on their assigned peg as soon as you're done with them makes it much easier to find them again.

The wrist pin is seen in its bronze bushing (bearing) on the connecting rod, a view not possible when this pin is positioned through its related piston.

FIVE EVENTS EQUAL ONE ENGINE CYCLE

A Depression-era flyer touting the superiority of Johnson Motor Company's outboard and washing machine motor construction really crystallized engine operation basics. In order for an internal combustion engine to run "and continuously deliver power," it noted, "the following routine of events must occur:

1. The engine cylinder must be supplied with a combustible mixture of air and gaseous fuel.
2. The gaseous mixture must be compressed or placed under pressure.
3. Ignition of the combustible mixture must take place.
4. A rapid rise in temperature will follow the [spark] firing of the combustible fuel, causing pressure and developing power.
5. The expulsion (scavenging) of burned gasses must take place, making way for the admission of the new combustible charge.

The accomplishment of these five acts is called a cycle of events, or commonly a cycle, and is performed differently in four-cycle motors than it is in two-cycle engines.

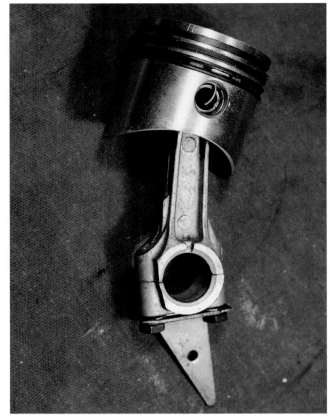

A four-stroker's piston/connecting rod assembly. The "keeper" spring (or snap ring) is evident at the end of the wrist pin. The triangle on the rod cap serves as an oil "dipper" that paddles crankcase oil onto appreciative moving parts.

mix ratios and oil type have differed, but every two-stroke maker devotes prime owner's manual space to warning of scored, scorched, or seized-up pistons and cylinders resulting from casual attention to such matters.

Be advised that because two-stroke mills covered in this book are of the air-cooled variety, they want a two-cycle oil formulated for air-cooled engines, as opposed to oils used in outboard motors, which are predominantly water-cooled and thus cooler running.

FOUR-CYCLE (OR FOUR-STROKE) OPERATION

Instead of the cylinder ports of two-stroke engines, four-strokers utilize mechanically activated valves to let fuel/air mixture into the cylinder and allow exhaust gases to exit. This type of motor takes four strokes of the piston to go through the five-event cycle outlined in the sidebar on this page. Stroke one of the process occurs when the piston travels downward and, via a cam driven by a gear meshed to another gear on the crankshaft, the *intake* valve is lifted open from its seat. This lets in fresh fuel/air mixture. In stroke two, the piston comes up and compresses the mixture in the area between the piston crown and top of the cylinder. Ignition motivates stroke three, via the power generated by exploding gases, driving the piston downward. And then, while going upward again, the piston—as mated to its connecting rod, which is ringed to the crankshaft, which is meshed to the camshaft gearing—pushes spent fuel/air gases out of the now-opened *exhaust* valve, so that stroke four can be accomplished.

Even if a four-stroke engine's spark plug is timed to ignite whenever the piston reaches its apex, or TDC, the fire during the exhaust stroke can't do much with gases that have already been burned. Consequently, four-stroke ignition is effective every second time the piston crown hits TDC. Compare this to a two-stroke mill's ignition occurring with each piston apex, and you can see how two-cycle buffs reason that their favorite type of motor packs twice the power punch of a four-cycle or "conventional automotive" engine.

FOUR-STROKE LUBRICATION

In addition to housing moving parts, the crankcase of a four-stroke motor is meant to serve as oil reservoir. Many small four-cycle engines are lubed via oil that's splashed into needed spots by way of a paddle arm or dipper affixed to the connecting rod end cap. Some use gear-driven pumps or scatter gear wheels to distribute oil to critical friction points.

When most of the vintage mills prevalent in the "used lawnmower" garage sale marketplace were originally manufactured, long-lasting synthetic motor oil was either in its experimental stage or a province of race car engines. Assuming that conventional oil is being used, Briggs & Stratton literature through the twentieth century recommended draining and changing the crankcase oil every 25 hours of engine operation. Running in dusty air necessitates shorter oil-change intervals. Like those of other makers, Briggs manuals warned small-engine owners that brand-new motors, or those run in very hot weather or under heavy loads, are likely to use more oil than engines babied in a nice environment. Key to good mechanical health, too, is ensuring that a four-stroker's crankcase is treated to clean oil right up to the optimum specified filler mark, whether measured on a little dipstick or a line on the fill neck. More than a few old-timers who enjoy several decades of trouble-free service from the engine on their garden tractor, snowblower, mower, or tiller attribute that great relationship to regular oil changes.

The piston from a two-cycle engine is shown with rings a bit out of their grooves. It's important that rings not get stuck, as it is "springiness" that allows them to do their work by creating a good compression seal for the piston inside the cylinder. Not evident here, but present in the ring grooves of many two-strokers, are little pins or up-ticks in the groove casting to keep the rings in a specific position. That way, the ring's ends can't move around to a cylinder port, where they would likely get caught, break off, and cause severe cylinder scoring.

Note the two piston rings as seen through the exhaust ports. The carbon buildup there needs to be cleaned away, or the engine will lose power. Most two-stroke buffs recommend making sure that, during cleaning, the piston is covering the ports (as shown), and that a Popsicle stick or plastic instrument be used to avoid scoring the piston.

TROUBLESHOOTING

My first experience with a balky small engine took place after I inadvertently tried cutting up a pile of rocks with our nearly new Briggs & Stratton–powered rotary mower. Actually, the stones had been well camouflaged by tall grass, so, as a sixth-grader, I was assured by my dad that the

A Lawn-Boy cutaway educational engine shows the piston in the down stroke position, uncovering the exhaust ports.

With the piston returned to near top dead center of its up stroke, the ever-smaller combustion area (in the cylinder) creates a good environment for compressing the fuel/air mix that the spark will ignite.

This two-cycle piston crown (above) needs some attention on the wire wheel to remove the carbon buildup and come out relatively sparkling. Be careful, though, when cleaning a carbonized piston, not to gouge or score, the sides or "skirt" area. The result is scan at right.

LET'S SEE WHAT THE MANUFACTURER SAYS ABOUT IT

Few motorheads can honestly claim that, while making small-engine repairs, they've never uttered the inquisitive phrase, "I wonder where the @!$% this part is supposed to go?" To curtail such frustrating experiences, the acquisition of a manufacturer's service manual is indispensable. Though online auction sites are good sources for such documents, the fat books can sometimes be secured very reasonably from local small-engine repair shops that are updating material, cleaning house, or calling it quits. Especially helpful in these (typically) snap-bound collections are line drawings of parts breakdowns for specific motors, model/year (and sometimes serial number) guides, and monthly factory-to-dealer service bulletins pinpointing modification and repair tips for problematic engines in particular serial number ranges. Most every motor maker published something of this ilk. Buffs who get a service manual once owned by some packrat proprietor often find rare product catalog sheets, promotional brochures (for everything from lighted dealers' signs to replacement muffler display counter stands), and engine invoices amid the more technical stuff.

Suffice it to say, the tomes contain lots of incredibly useful (and historical) inside information originally intended only for the eyes of those in the motor maker's franchised dealer and service centers. When buying a resource like the pictured *Clinton Master Parts & Service Manual* (4 inches thick and stuffed with about 15 pounds of pages), pay particular attention to the content's date range to be sure it covers your era of interest. Additionally, unless it's a freebie, beware of empty file tab sections that might have contained details that a similar manual—put together by a more organized shop owner—would have included.

Manufacturers' service manuals contain lots of incredibly useful information originally intended only for the eyes of those in the motor maker's franchised dealer and service centers.

motor's maladies were not my fault. The following Saturday, he dropped off me and the mower at a local small-engine repair shop, housed in a former farm shed in back of the curmudgeonly proprietor's home. This gave me a chance to watch the old guy quietly operate and an opportunity to ask a few questions about what he was doing between his pet phrases like "That don't look so good" and "OK, close enough for government work."

Recognizing Something's Out of Whack
"Mister, whaddaya think is wrong with it?" I ventured. He turned and slowly began with a bit of small talk (asking

what I wanted to do when I grew up, etc.) and pointedly queried why we'd brought the Briggs to him in the first place. "Well, it stopped because the blade ran over some rocks, and then I couldn't get it going again because the starter cord pulls real hard and slow."

"Good," he nodded, "you've learned the first useful thing about troubleshooting small engines: Before anything can be fixed, you need to understand that it's broke."

Proper English not withstanding, the old fellow made a valid point. He supported it with several tales of 3-horsepower "patients" brought to his small-engine hospital that could have avoided surgery had their owners paid some

THE OLD CRAFTSMAN DRILL PRESS—A METAPHOR FOR SMALL-ENGINE RESTORATION

Shortly after agreeing to write this book, I took delivery on a pretty weary and wiggly 1950s Craftsman drill press acquired in an eBay auction. It came just in time for me to restore the vintage Sears product (actually built for the famed retailer by King-Seeley Corporation) for use in several small jobs related to engine projects covered in Chapter 4. According to the seller's eBay description, it was "in nice shape, needing nothing but maybe a quick clean up (if the new owner cares about looks) and a replacement drive belt." Instead, the heavy old cast-iron ugly duckling and ⅓-horse Dunlap ball bearing electric motor told the rusty tale of having been left outdoors in a nearly defunct New Jersey boatyard. In an effort to ameliorate my disappointment, I resolved to treat it to the same revitalizing process offered to a prized small engine. That is to say, the classic Craftsman drill press soon underwent disassembly and cleaning and degreasing with solvent and the wire wheel to find a good surface for eventual repainting. In addition, its motor received a thorough cleaning and repaint, and was rewired with a new switch and industrial electrical cord and plug, as opposed to the jerry-rigged wiring rat's nest and frayed lamp cord that dubiously led to the device's primary and secondary windings. Following the application of fresh gray paint and clear sealer to the proud little "Craftsman, Guaranteed Highest Quality" nameplate, the unit's now-shiny moving parts were oiled and reinstalled. Some serendipitously discovered scrap oak fit perfectly on the press table to finish off the project. I was so anxious to try out this now-beautiful swan that I refitted it with the old chewed-up drive belt—the only part that the former owner figured needed attention. The Craftsman redux turned out to be an enjoyably useful success. Meanwhile, the belt performs admirably, but admittedly needs replacement so that this project can be considered officially completed.

A 1950s Craftsman drill press *as found. Even the motor drive pulley is warped.*

Just as one would do to begin a motor restoration, the component systems are separated and later dismantled.

While all parts—especially the internal moving components—were cleaned on the wire wheel (above), the author treated the Craftsman drill press head casting to a fresh coat of paint (below). By suspending the casting from a wire, the paint can be conveniently applied.

Don't tell the fire marshal, but after separating and dismantling the component systems, we poured gasoline into a pie tin and then used a gas-soaked rag to effectively degrease the parts. That paintbrush helped get the solvent into nooks and crannies.

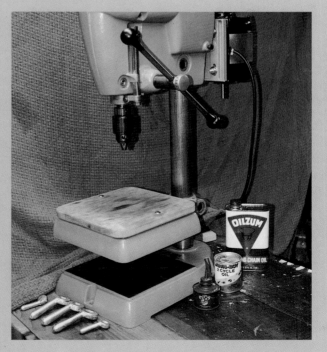

The restored machine is ready for service in the small-engine shop. The handles are cast-aluminum reproductions of originals.

Two views of flywheel-mounted magnets in a magneto system, one inside and the other embedded on the outer perimeter. Both have "keepers" on them while off their respective motors. Though rife with rust and broken cooling-fan blades, that flywheel holding the bolt and 3/4-inch socket shows off its magnetism. Technically, the socket feat is sufficient proof that those magnets are OK.

Upside-down perspective of a four-stroke engine's cylinder head, with the spark plug hole and threads evident. The associated head gasket helps provide a good seal to the cylinder top. If the gasket is shrunk, thinned, ripped, or otherwise deficient, or if the head surface is not perfectly flat, compression will suffer. Check for flatness by placing the head on a known flat surface (like plate glass) and trying to slide a piece of paper (or feeler gauge element) under it.

On magnetos with outside flywheel magnets, access is possible for inspecting specific spacing between flywheel and coil heels. Typically .010 of an inch—or the thickness of a business card—will do the trick. If out of tolerance, the coil assembly can be repositioned.

attention to symptomatic overheating, sluggish rpm, squeaks, and knocking noises that desperately signaled low oil levels.

Meeting Needs: Fuel? Compression? Spark?
He had me help lift the lawnmower onto a rough oak workbench intricately splotched with variously shaped oil stains.

Next, he stood back to survey the engine, as if being able to direct some X-ray vision through its crankcase. "Let's see if your Briggs is getting what she needs," he mumbled. Amused that he figured our engine to be female, I wondered aloud how one could assign gender to a motor, and was curious as to *her* requirements.

"If your dad and mom didn't tell you about the birds and

The throttle governor vane is blown by air from the cooling fans and consequently regulates speed. Note that the spark plug wire has been removed from the plug. This should be the first order of business whenever working on small engines (unless, of course, you're trying to test for spark).

With guts removed, this crankcase (above left) exposes its cylinder bore (large hole) and bronze bushing (bearing) in which a crankshaft end smoothly rides. The groove and hole in the bearing allow for oil flow. That little slice of dark metal between aluminum ridges (above right) is a telltale sign that this otherwise all-aluminum engine has a cast-iron sleeve-cylinder bore. Briggs & Stratton pioneered the process to offer a compromise between a heavy cast-iron block motor and one with an aluminum cylinder. Briggs dubbed its all-aluminum versions "Kool-Bore," and those treated to a cast-iron sleeve "Sleeve-Bore."

THE CASE OF THE WHISTLING SNOWBLOWER

The cardboard sign on the Ariens ST-504 read, "Needs TLC . . . $40." We pulled in the driveway and listened to the seller's story. "It ran real good for lots of winters," he fondly recalled, "but I just bought a new machine because the old one started giving me a little trouble." When my son asked about the symptoms, the fellow said that it began whistling and eventually stopped working altogether. "Did it whistle anything in particular?" we asked incredulously. The owner didn't think the whistle sounded like a specific song, just a funny little boiling teapot. He also admitted not knowing much about engines, though he believed the carburetor might be making the noise because it was loose. The fellow then remembered tightening the carb bowl screw. "And that's when the poor thing bit the dust . . . or snow," he chuckled. He then offered us the vintage Ariens with its Tecumseh Snow King motor for half the sign's asking price.

Our $20 acquisition wore a surprising amount of fuzz, the result of its former master's cats rubbing themselves on it in his walkout basement. After a general cleaning, the Tecumseh's fuel tank and line were emptied and cleaned. The spark was still potent, so we quickly turned our attention to the main suspect. That Tecumseh-built float-bowl carburetor seemed relieved to finally be getting diagnostic attention. What a mistreated mess it was! Antique gas had slicked the float and associated parts with a smelly, gooey green varnish that demanded ample sprays of choke and carburetor cleaner. Somehow the throttle's butterfly valve got jammed into the fast position. It was during our refitting of this piece that we noticed a lot of play in the shaft on which the throttle valve pivots to open and closed. In fact, the shaft hole in the top of the carburetor was sufficiently worn to quite possibly cause passing intake air to whistle through the carb, though we never detected such tune weaving. And what of the tightened carburetor bowl screw? Well, rather than being an actual bowl fastener, as the previous owner thought, this screw was a needle valve that choked off fuel when turned down to

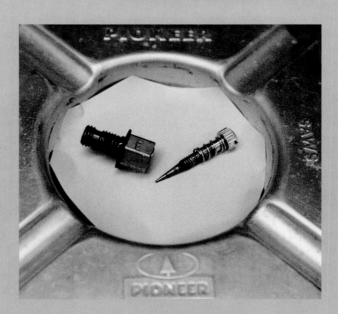

the fully seated position. Gently dressing the ridges that suffered upon being impacted into the seat put the needle valve in usable shape and joined the other repairs that motivated the Snow King to start humming again. Following a winter's workout, it was sold for 50 bucks to an enterprising girl down the street during an early snowstorm the following December. When I protested to my son that he should have simply given the old Ariens to the cute little kid, he shrugged that she'd already used the darn thing to clear a half-dozen neighborhood driveways, making $120 in a day—quite probably whistling while she and the trusty Tecumseh worked.

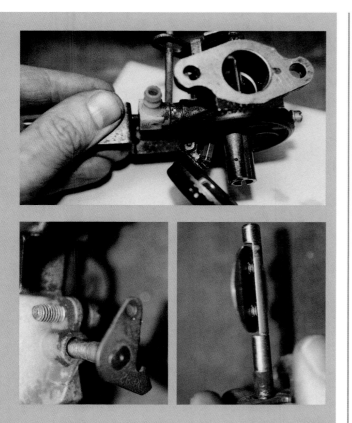

Opposite top: Cat fuzz has invaded this poor Tecumseh's carburetor intake. Opposite middle: Note the throttle butterfly valve jammed open. Somehow its top fitting got lodged against the mounting flange. The screw allegedly holding on the carburetor bowl (at bottom) is actually a needle valve. Opposite bottom: It was the needle-valve seat nut, not the needle-valve screwhead, that the former owner should have tightened. The needle valve did suffer a bit of ridging from being too snug, though a delicate sanding smoothed it out sufficiently. Top: A 1956 AC Spark Plugs booklet, Hints on the Care and Feeding of Small Engines, indicates, "if your engine stands for more than a week without being used, gum may form in the carburetor. Adding two tablespoonfuls of lacquer thinner to each gallon of gas will help prevent gum clogging." Obviously, this carb was stored full of what became very old gas. When that evaporated, it left significant varnish deposits to gum up the float, float valve, and other intricate parts. Spray-on carburetor cleaner and a bath in an erstwhile cottage cheese container filled with lacquer thinner aided in the necessary cleaning. Be advised that both of the aforementioned solvents will dull or remove paint, decals, and lettering on motor identification tags. Keep it away from any finish you want to preserve. Above left: Look closely at the hole through which the throttle butterfly valve protrudes. If you can see the little air space between the two, you've detected why the carburetor whistled while it worked. Above right: It turned out that the butterfly valve post (on which the butterfly is loosely screwed) was worn where it fit into the carburetor body. It needed replacement so that air coming through the carb wouldn't escape.

bees yet, I ain't gonna," he pledged, "but everybody knows women are more complicated than men. So don't it make sense to say a four-cycle engine—endowed with valves, tappets, valve springs, and a camshaft—is more intricate than two-strokers that just use ports for their intake and exhaust, and so should be addressed as a little lady?"

Seconds after asking what our girl needed, I was amused by my instructor's rhythmic mantra, "*Fuel, compression, spark*." Each was explained in a fashion similar to this chapter's previous sections. "Never shy away from checking for the most obvious problems first," he noted, "even if they don't seem too fancy." And then we tested for them.

The *fuel* was fresh, and its tank and associated line both proved clean and a clear pathway to the crankcase. With the cylinder head removed and flywheel rotated, we could see the valves open and close at correct intervals. And a check of the carb showed no signs of leakage either related to fuel dribbling out or to stray air getting in. With those components each having passed the test, we could safely say that the fuel system didn't seem to be presenting a problem.

Neither was cylinder *compression* suspect, as the needle on an air pressure gauge he'd threaded into the spark plug hole registered well within the acceptable range (though he really had to struggle with the starter cord to obtain a reading) according to a thick, greasy fingerprint–laden service manual held open by a rusty camshaft from a previous job.

Spark, however, was another story. Though he'd devoted his full strength to cranking over the engine to get a compression reading, the repairman had me tug the starter handle while he checked for a telltale spark plug flash. There was negligible fire. "Interesting case," came a whispered pronouncement just loud enough for me to hear and to intensify my curiosity. "The ignition system is fine," he noted, "except for something not letting you pull fast enough to generate a good spark."

If Something Isn't Working, Why Not?

I'm pretty sure the repairman knew all along what the problem was, as he wanted me to try identifying a noise that we first noticed while pulling the cord moments after my dad wheeled the ailing mower into the shop. "Hear that?" He pointed, and then roped it over again.

"Sounds like something metal is rubbing on metal . . . like something's too tight," was my simplistic diagnosis. We had already drained the gas tank before the aforementioned carb inspection and made sure the oil filler cap was tight after checking for an acceptable lube level (which looked a bit low), so everything proved ready for flipping the mower and engine on its side. Along with the shop's ample lighting, this gave us a great perspective to see that some oil had

Here's a crankshaft seal. Like other seals designed to keep oil and compression inside the engine while guarding against outside air, water, and dirt, it comprises synthetic rubber (or plastic) and associated (typically metal) mounting assembly. This seal rides next to the main crankshaft bearing.

The air-cleaner (filter) assembly for a 1960s Clinton uses a foam rubber element. Sometimes, when this material gets old, it decomposes or breaks apart, resulting in particles inside the very carburetor it is designed to keep clean.

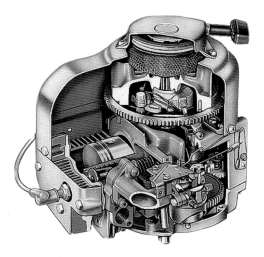

A four-cycle Lauson/Tecumseh cutaway. Courtesy Tecumseh Archives

A Tecumseh four-stroke display piece fitted with overhead valves. Courtesy Tecumseh Products Corp.

There's your trouble! The white Tecumseh snowblower engine blew its connecting rod through the crankcase when its piston suddenly seized in the cylinder and broke off the connecting rod. "I guess I should have seen if there was any oil in the motor," its owner surmised after only getting to clear half of his driveway in a blizzard. A two-stoker with too little oil in the fuel mix suffered a similar fate as this sad piston/connecting rod.

THE QUICKIE TUNE-UP

Just like "deluxe accommodations," the term "tune-up" has varying degrees of meaning depending on the speaker's background. For our purposes, we'll define "tune-up" as *the noninvasive procedure that refreshes a small engine.* The "noninvasive" part might be somewhat misstated, though, as shrouding and flywheel removal is often required to service the ignition system. In any event, our prescriptive procedure starts with a serious cleaning of the motor's exterior, and then moves on to these measures:

Clean or replace air filter.

Clean carburetor. This may include dropping the bowl and getting rid of any sediment. Also possible in this step is the removal of the main (high-speed) and idle jets. Clean and return them to their suggested settings. If the carburetor is suspect, replace gaskets and diaphragm or float-related components as contained in the make and model's "carburetor kit," typically available at major auto parts stores, lawn and power-equipment shops, or from large retailers. A new needle-valve seat and related packing gasket may provide a major cure for carb trouble.

Clean or replace crankcase breather. Some breathers use a reed valve. Be careful not to bend the reeds out of factory tolerances.

Clean or replace (and gap with feeler gauge) spark plug. Inspect magneto–spark plug wire for fraying, splits, or breaks. Replace if damaged.

Check condenser (or simply replace).

Clean (dress with fine sandpaper) ignition points. Set points as per manufacturer's specs.

Clean away any grass, dirt, or debris from fan blades and fan screen.

Change oil (on a four-stroke).

Replace old fuel with fresh.

dribbled from the crankshaft seal, down the end of the crank, and onto the top of the mower blade. I started to rotate the blade when the shop owner firmly stated, "Wait! Are you sure that the magneto wire is removed from the spark plug?" While popping the rubber cap off the plug contact, he recounted a tale of an engine in such a position starting up when some novice mechanic spun its blade and got seriously injured. "Bad business," the fellow instructed. "A real day spoiler!"

Once the plug wire was safely grounded, the minilecture quickly transitioned into his hand motion prompting me

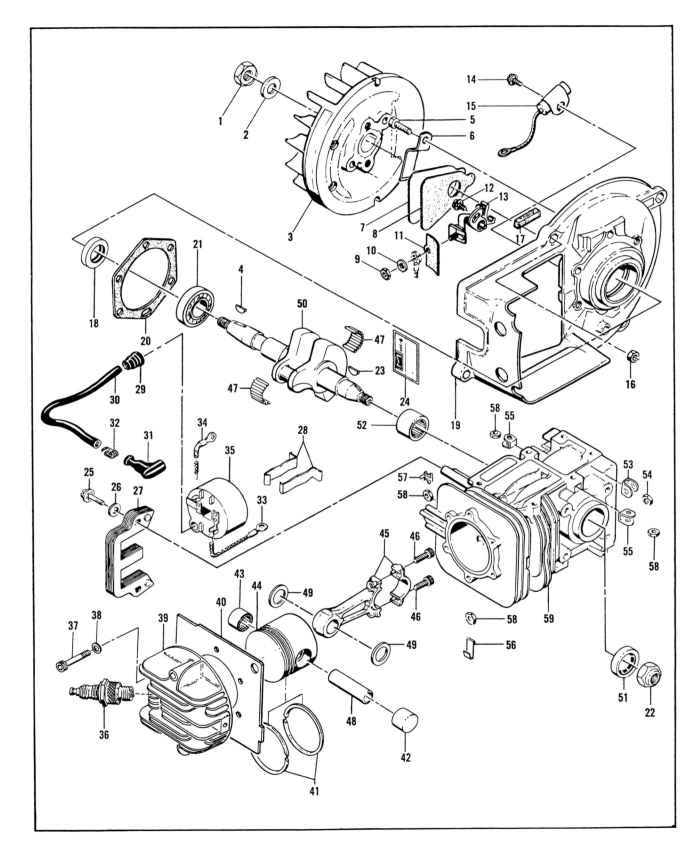

FIGURE 3. POWERHEAD ASSEMBLY   MC-6

Index No.	Part Number	Nomenclature	Units Per Assy
3-1	101179	Nut - Hex 7/16-20	1
-2	101270	Washer - Special	1
-3	48785	Flywheel Assy	1
-4	100199	Key - Woodruff No. 3	1
-5	55494	Sealing Screw - Hex hd	6
-6	50671	Retainer - Breaker box cover	1
-7	50588	Cover - Breaker box	1
-8	50589	Gasket - Breaker box	1
-9	100251	Nut - Hex 8-32	1
-10	100057	Lockwasher - Internal No. 8	1
-11	50381	Insulator - Breaker terminal	1
-12	103672	Screw - Fil hd 8-32 x 1/2 in. lg (Sems)	1
-13	50076A	Breaker Assy	1
-14	103672	Screw - Fil hd 8-32 x 1/2 in. lg (Sems)	1
-15	50074	Condenser	1
—	57126	Crankcase Cover Assy	1
-16	101326	. Nut - Hex 10-24	2
-17	54184	. Wiper - Crankcase cover felt	1
-18	50663	. Oil Seal - Crankcase	1
-19		. Cover - Crankcase (Order Crankcase Cover Assy #57126)	1
-20	51240	Gasket - Crankcase cover	1
-21	100824	Bearing - Ball	1
-22	103746	Locknut - Hex 3/8-24	1
-23	100199	Key - Woodruff No. 3	1
-24	48799	Nameplate	1
-25	104138	Screw - Hex hd 10-24 x 7/8 in. lg (Sems)	2
-26	102189	Washer - Plain No. 10	2
-27	51251	Lamination Assy	1
-28	51253	Retainer - Coil	2
—	55973	Coil and Terminal Assy	1
-29	55617	. Nipple	1
-30	52547	. Wire Assy - Spark plug	1
-31	55060	. . Boot - Spark plug	1
-32	55061	. . Connector	1
-33	101883	. Wire Assy - Ground	1
-34	50137	. Wire Assy - Primary	1
-35		. Coil Assy (Order Coil and Terminal Assy #55973)	1
-36		Plug - Spark 14-mm (J-4J or equivalent)	1
-37	101563	Screw - Socket hd 10-24 x 1-1/4 in. lg	6
-38	24236	Washer - Plain No. 10	6
-39	55146A	Head - Cylinder	1
-40	48816	Gasket - Cylinder head	1
—	48844	Piston Assy	1
-41	48691	. Ring Set - Piston (Two rings - top ring chrome)	1
-42	104378	. Bearing - Closed end	1
-43	101206	. Bearing	1
-44		. Piston (Order Piston Assy #48844)	1
-45	55009	Connecting Rod Assy	1
-46	101356	. Screw - Socket hd 10-32 x 5/8 in. lg	2
-47	102742	. Roller - Needle	24
-48	57198	Pin - Piston	1
-49	51209	Washer - Thrust	2
-50	48744	Crankshaft	1
	48701	Crankcase Assy	1
-51	104128	. Oil Seal	1
-52	104129	. Bearing - Needle	1
-53	18556A	. Retainer - Nut	4
-54	101143	. Locknut - Hex 1/4-20	4
-55	28053	. Retainer - Nut	2
-56	57063	. Retainer - Nut	4
-57	104255	. Retainer - Nut	2
-58	101326	. Locknut - Hex 10-24	8
-59		. Crankcase (Order Crankcase Assy #48701)	1

Whenever delving into a small motor, it's extremely helpful to have the make and model's factory "illustrated parts list" to clearly discern where everything goes—or went, in the case of missing pieces. Here are a couple of crucial pages for a 1960 McCulloch MC-6 kart engine.

The outside of that little Briggs tank looked good, but a glance inside revealed a rusty tale of water (perhaps from condensation) in the gas. Actually, the gasoline had long since evaporated, leaving stuff like this to either get cleaned out or clogged in the fuel system. Revitalizing a tank's interior take lots of elbow grease . . . and a few pebbles, bolts, or nuts to agitate the crud loose.

Sometimes things just aren't right, even when new. This incredibly marred piston was removed from a garden tractor engine that the customer complained "wouldn't run at all." The factory quickly covered the cost of a new engine. Without much sign (on the piston crown and exhaust valve) that the motor was ever fired up, the dealer and factory rep were both puzzled as to the cause of the piston's damage—especially since its related cylinder bore was fine.

And then there's the case of the new engine with a rusty overhead valve. Ready for the solution? A careless kid working after school at his local power-equipment shop spilled his sports drink all over a snowblower while he was "prepping" the engine—minus its sparkplug. The unit was sold the following spring to a bargain-hunting clearance-sale shopper who didn't discover the trouble until the next winter.

This four-stroker was inexplicably partially jammed until it was discovered that its end cap had been installed upside down, causing the end-cap bolts to impact the crankcase.

A vital "repair" that any lawnmower owner can make is to clean the accumulated grass clippings from the mower deck. This prolongs the mower's life and is especially helpful for engines that have underdeck exhaust. Be sure the spark plug wire has been disconnected and watch out for leaking fuel when the unit is flipped over.

to again try rotating the crankshaft via the blade. "It looks and feels like it's bent," I offered. He seemed pleased with my assessment, then pointed to the lower crankcase seal and bearing. "And there's signs of oil leaking from that part," was my reply. This netted me his verification that indeed the crank had been bent when its associated moving blade slammed into those immovable rocks. "That leaked oil is there because the bang buggered up the bearing and seal, in the process," the veteran technician pronounced. "Now, what do you think we can do for her?"

Deciding How to Solve the Problem

The fact that a bent crank, made of hardened steel, could be straightened surprised me. Fortunately, though, the shop was equipped with a hydraulic press capable of exerting the force necessary to right the component. "We could order a new crank from Briggs & Stratton," the avuncular proprietor mused, "but your dad probably don't wanna spend that kind of dough. The bearing and seal is a different kettle of fish, though." He rummaged through an old wooden cabinet. "Got a new one in stock here somewhere. So that's what we'll do . . . straighten her crank and fit the little gal

Removing the cowling of a garage sale chainsaw gives quick access to the air filter. A clean one is a sign of a fastidious owner or little use. The flywheel fan and cylinder-cooling fins can be inspected for excessive dirt or sawdust. A fast spark test (if someone has a wrench handy) is in order, too.

with a new bearing."

"She'll like that," I smiled, and waited to see if the guy would let me assist in the operation.

Making Things Right

After we drained the crankcase oil, my engine repair teacher instructed as I removed screws holding the cowling/rewind starter in place. "Don't ever fool with a bum rewind unit,"

In the 1970s Champion distribute this instructive spark plug condition/causes chart to anyone who repairs engines.

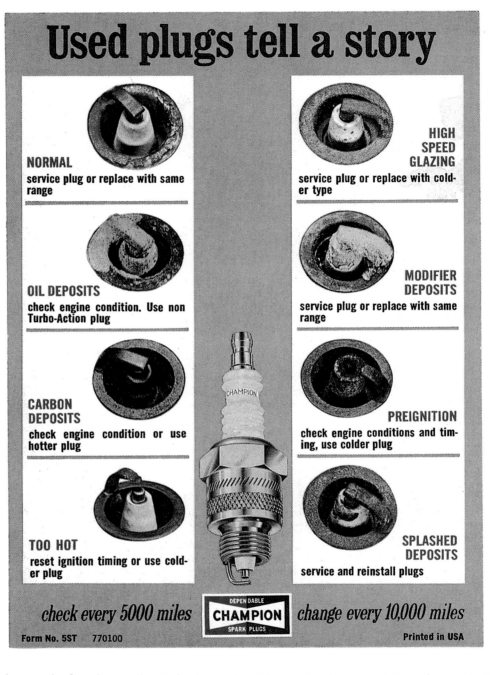

Used plugs tell a story

NORMAL
service plug or replace with same range

OIL DEPOSITS
check engine condition. Use non Turbo-Action plug

CARBON DEPOSITS
check engine condition or use hotter plug

TOO HOT
reset ignition timing or use colder plug

HIGH SPEED GLAZING
service plug or replace with colder type

MODIFIER DEPOSITS
service plug or replace with same range

PREIGNITION
check engine conditions and timing, use colder plug

SPLASHED DEPOSITS
service and reinstall plugs

check every 5000 miles   **CHAMPION** DEPENDABLE SPARK PLUGS   *change every 10,000 miles*

Form No. 5ST   770100   Printed in USA

he warned, "unless you got on gloves and safety glasses. The rewinder's tightly wound spring can whip your face real bad."

Next, I took out nuts and bolts that allowed us to get at the motor's innards. "Careful, now, careful," he whispered on several occasions while directing the steps that finally led to extricating the damaged crankshaft. Along the way, he had me thoughtfully group the removed components in a couple of trays, each lined with a red shop rag. "That way," the fellow indicated from years of experience, "we stand a better chance of knowing where stuff is and how it goes

back together. It's amazing how easy it is to forget which thing goes where, even an hour after you take it apart."

A special removal tool—simply a two-step metal dowel with a lip several inches from the narrow end that was almost as wide as the bearing's outer diameter—allowed the shop owner to pop out the offending bearing. After being satisfied that the aluminum crankcase hadn't suffered in the rock incident, he installed the new bearing. And the crank responded well enough to his press to be judged "good enough for government work."

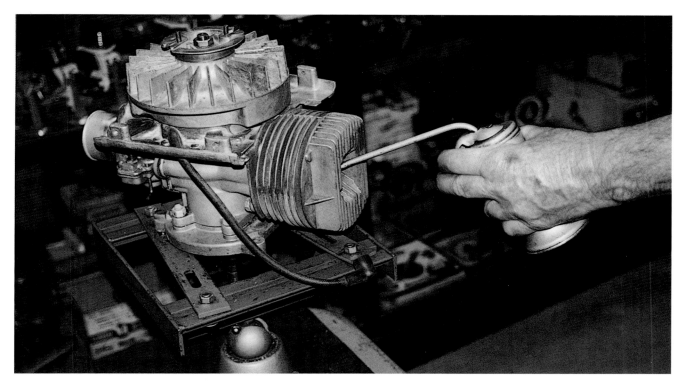

Whenever a small engine will be at rest for at least several weeks, a shot of oil in the cylinder is great insurance against rust, corrosion, and undue friction.

Wear protective glasses when wire wheel–brushing parts, as they have a tendency to fly off of the pliers. Treating a handful of bolts to a wire wheel is time-consuming but the best way to go when preparing to put an engine back together. Laying out the different screw, washer, nut, and bolt denominations makes things handy for reassembly.

Driving through a piston pin via a curved wooden block designed to nicely cradle the piston is a lot less frustrating than having it clumsily roll around during the process.

Before removing the end cap from its connecting rod, mark two matching edges with a prick punch so you'll recall which side goes to which. That's a step that's well worth the effort.

A Final Check

I recall one bolt being left over following the surgery. After searching for its home and hoping he wouldn't order me to take everything apart again, and then confessing that I had no idea where the darn thing was supposed to go, my motor mentor smiled and gestured toward a junked Clinton two-stroke kart mill "some spoiled rich kid with more money than brains fried" by neglecting to add oil to the gas. "While you weren't paying attention," he chuckled, "I took it off that poor thing and put it in your parts tray. See, it's got traces of Clinton red paint, and the Briggs is kinda an off-white. Remember, it don't hurt to be more observant whenever you're performing open *part* surgery. Now, let's check our compression again and feel if the crank turns nice and smooth in her new bearing."

Some gas and a can of oil later, we rolled the mower outside and I got the honor of yanking the starter handle. Fully choked, she sprang to life in the middle of the second pull. We listened for abnormal noises at high-speed to idle, and were satisfied that all was audibly well. The proprietor then killed the ignition so we could flip the mower upward to inspect for oil leaking past the new bearing. He cautioned about dripping gas on the hot muffler before looking at what turned out to be a nice clean lower main-bearing exterior. The "warm engine" test—to be certain that it'd restart easily—was in progress when Dad returned from his errands. "Sounds like it's working fine," my father grinned.

"It's not an *it*, it's a *she*," I protested. "All four-strokers are like complicated women or something like that."

"And it sounds like my son has been receiving a wide variety of insights," Dad noted with a bit of suspicion in his voice. "What do I owe you for parts and labor?"

The old mechanic used a forefinger to scribble a few imaginary numbers in the air. "Uh, a buck-eighty-seven for the bearing, seal, some oil, and tax," he announced. "No charge for the labor, because my assistant here did the work. Besides," the guy reflected, "your boy tells me he'd like to write books someday, so maybe he can write one about small engines and put me in it."

Use a lapping stick to twirl a valve in lapping compound in order to "grind" a better seat.

A valve-seat cutter is positioned into a valve-seat area that needs its angle better matched to the valve face.

An electric drill drives a cylinder hone designed to create a fine surface pattern on a cylinder wall in need of an improved finish—especially after a reboring. Sanding with fine-grit paper and then cleaning with solvent on a cloth should complete the job. Because the piston rings never contact the uppermost portion of the cylinder, the area with no appreciable wear (called the "ring ridge") needs to be honed flush with the rest of the cylinder. Often, this requires the use of a "ridge reamer" tool.

CHAPTER 4
CASE STUDIES

A VINTAGE TWO-STROKER GETS ONE MORE CHANCE: LAWN-BOY LAWN-CRUISER

"Hey buddy," somebody at an old-engine swap meet whispered to me as if possessing a top military secret, "I hear you might be looking for a classic Lawn-Boy motor to fix up for, shall we say, an important project. He'd eavesdropped on me telling another winter show attendee that I was searching for a simple but well-built two-cycle, air-cooled single to feature in this book. Of course, the guy just happened to know where one could obtain such a vintage mill . . . for, shall we say, a reasonable price. An hour or so later, I found myself on the north side of the U.S.-Canadian border staring at a snow-capped mound of mechanical mish-mash next to one of the fellow's many sheds. "Take your pick, they're all beauties," he declared of the 20 or so Lawn-Boy mowers comprising that corroded pile.

"Well," began my assessment of the selection, "I was actually hoping to find one that doesn't have ice in the gas tank. Do you have any of those quintessential Lawn-Boy

This poor, pitiful little Lawn-Cruiser 18 looks like it's resigned to spending another winter parked in snow under a Canadian porch. Later, after I saved it from such a fate and unloaded the two-stroke mower in my driveway, a skeptical neighbor quipped, "Tell me you didn't pay good money for that rusty, cracked piece of junk."

Cleaning with a whiskbroom and shop vacuum is the best way to start any mechanical fix-up, revitalization, or full restoration.

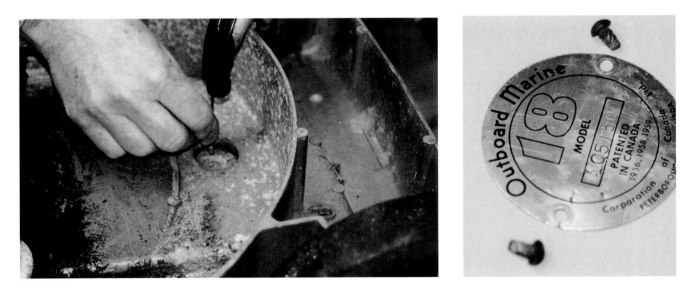

Use a pin punch tool underneath the mower deck to remove the fasteners that hold the all-important nametag.

CASE STUDIES

mowers with the engine mounted on the deck sideways?"

"Oh," he smiled slyly, "You're looking for the *good* stuff." Directing me to follow him under the weathered deck of his house, he ceremoniously pulled an old beach towel from the powerhead of an otherwise snow-covered lawnmower, unveiling the Lawn-Boy engine model I wanted. "It's a classic Iron Horse motor," he stated solemnly. "Been in the family for decades. We call it 'old faithful' and use it to cut our grass all summer long. Don't know if the wife and kids would be willing to let me part with this sweet antique."

Fifty American dollars later, I wheeled the Lawn-Boy through 2 inches of recent snowfall, wrestled off its push

Carefully removing the Iron Horse–embossed rewind starter revealed evidence of rust and corrosion (that white stuff) that needed removal. Fortunately, the poor performance of the rewind starter was remedied by applying oil to the mechanism and giving the rope a vigorous workout.

handle, and stuffed the thing into the trunk of my car. Finally home, I reversed the process and instantly noticed that nothing on the entire unit officially said Lawn-Boy; rather, the embossed moniker Lawn-Cruiser jumped out at me. That's always the way it goes, though. No matter how intricately you inspect an old engine, the process of actually purchasing it and carting it home will cause you

A strap wrench sure makes loosening the flywheel nut a lot easier than would be the case if you tried to hold the flywheel still with a spare hand.

A compression tester and a good strong yank on the starter cord helps determine the general health of the pistons, rings, crankcase-to-cylinder gasket, and cylinder. Be sure to ground the spark plug wire whenever cranking the engine over for such an exam.

to immediately see previously and mysteriously invisible defects or contradictions. In this case, observations made once the Lawn-Cruiser was irrevocably in my shop included noticing that the engine's fuel tank was caked with significant internal rust. That would have made little difference, however, as the fuel line between tank and carburetor was long gone anyway. And a test for spark revealed total darkness. In conducting the exam, I pulled on the starter cord, causing its related ratchets to clunk a refusal to rewind for another try. So much for the Lawn-Cruiser having recently beautified any yard.

On the positive side of the Lawn-Cruiser's ledger, at least it wasn't stuck. When freed from the starter mechanism, its flywheel delivered a healthy compression bounce, declaring

Having taken off the flywheel, we get our first look at the magneto. Someone along the way cut out a section of the points protector, but otherwise it seems complete and workable.

that the cylinder, piston, and rings were all in good order. A second twist of the wrist generated enough compression to cause the reed valves to sing out a nice "chirp" characteristic of two-strokers with decent guts.

By this time, I was beginning to feel a bit better about my acquisition. Though also faced with a long crack in the mower deck, I reasoned that such challenges would only add character to this story, and I rushed to the shop shelves in search of a Lawn-Boy service manual. Strangely, none of the book's thousand pages specifically referenced this mower model, the LC-5150. Even though it listed a similar-looking Midland-branded, badge-engineered Lawn-Boy mower for 1960, there wasn't a single sentence about the Lawn-Cruiser marque. The engine's identification tag pegged the motor as a C-12B, serial number 709979. Its associated mower deck was labeled Outboard Marine Corporation of Canada, Ltd. Patent dates were 1956, 1958, and 1959, so the Lawn-Cruiser was likely a circa-1960 product. My references don't mention a C-12B, but do list a C-12 in 1956 and 1957 with a 2-horsepower rating at 3,200 rpm. For 1958, the C-12 series was upgraded to 2½ horsepower (under the C-12AAM and C-12AA designations—for use on Snow-Boy snowblowers in 1960 and 1961, respectively—the 2½ horses come from 4,000 rpm). Because private-brand products (those nominally disguised by their makers and typically sold to bargain hunters through discount or catalog stores) were often slightly outdated versions of the manufacturer's name-brand line, we

Off comes the interesting Lawn-Boy-type governor. Several photos were taken of this unit so that reassembly wouldn't be completely puzzling.

We probably should have removed the mower blade immediately after the initial powerhead cleaning. Note the deliberately loose spark plug wire between the wheels. Never spin a blade if there's any chance at all that the engine could start or even fire momentarily and injure the mechanic.

Nuts and bolts that have been exposed to the great outdoors must be cleaned with a wire brush in order to prepare their corners to accept a wrench.

With the muffler casting out of the way, we can do a cursory inspection of the exhaust ports and piston skirt. Rotate the crankshaft so that the piston is covering the ports. Had there been lots of carbonization and other goo in the ports, they'd need cleaning. These, however, appear to be surprisingly free of buildup.

After being lifted off its deck (right), the little two-stroker receives a basic workout with handheld wire brushes (below). The goal is to rid fins, flat areas, crevices, and nooks of corrosion so the motor can be returned as close to its bare-metal "factory" finish as possible. Keen observers might notice a bit of cloth protruding from the spark plug hole and exhaust porting to protect them from debris invasion. Had the carburetor not still been wearing its air filter, a "gag" rag would have been advisable in the carb opening, too.

Solvents may be applied to the powerhead with a paintbrush to loosen hard-baked dirt and grease. Obviously, this is outside work.

CASE STUDIES

can assume that the Lawn-Cruiser hails from 1960 and wears a 2-horsepower (or possibly a 2½-horse rating) Canadian OMC Lawn-Boy motor. Whatever the precise chronology, the mower's Lawn-Boy lineage and boldly embossed Lawn-Cruiser deck made it a neat nostalgic restoration project.

The process moved forward with a small brush and shop vacuum used to clear the engine and mower of wet leaves and dirt that had already led to some corrosion. As soon as the motor was freed from the deck it had called home for nearly 45 years, the awkwardness of how to hold a vertical-shaft engine while disassembling much of it presented a problem. Common sense suggests that the motor could best be handled on its deck, but that piece needed to be moved to another shop bench for reconstructive and cosmetic surgery. At first, the Lawn-Cruiser team braced

Rewinder, shrouding, and fuel tank await treatment. The tank was so rust-infested that we resorted to partially filling it with muriatic acid that mercilessly ate away the rust. Active liquids like acid, however, should not be used casually or by folks unsure of the stuff's chemical aggressiveness.

After the wheels took their leave, the mower deck got a general cleaning with "painted on" gasoline that was allowed to do its thing before being "rinsed off" (with more gas) and then dried with rags.

the engine's crankshaft end between two blocks of wood in a vise, but later decided to obtain a commercial stand intended for small-engine hospitals. In this device, the C-12B mill was easily accessible, plus we regained the use of the shop vise. Quicker and easier than anticipated, the flywheel came off. We didn't even need a puller for the task, though we kept it handy for another patient to be chronicled later in this chapter.

Removal of the flywheel offered an opportunity to test the magnets inside by placing a ¼-inch socket there to see if the magnetic force held it securely. It did, so we shifted attention to the rest of the ignition system. Someone had cut the plastic cover meant to protect the ignition points. We wondered why until noticing that the points were replacements (probably from a slightly different Lawn-Boy engine) that almost, but didn't quite fit under the housing.

The OMC-built powerhead is ready to undergo surgery.

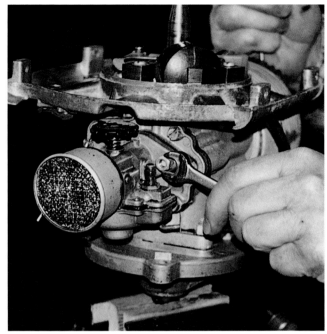

Undoing one of the two carb nuts.

Sometimes those miniscule washers are best extracted and reintroduced with tweezers.

The reed-plate assembly. Its two reeds bend in slightly toward the crankcase to allow fuel/air entry from the carburetor, which is typically positioned on the reed plate's front side. Crankcase compression back toward the reeds pushes them against the reed plate to prevent the fuel/air from going back to the carburetor.

With the reed-plate assembly gone, we can easily see the crankcase, connecting rod end cap, and crankshaft throws. Everything looks clean, and the fit felt appropriately within tolerance when we rotated the crankshaft.

Extracting the air filter screening material. Nowadays, foam makes for popular air filtration, but this stuff was typical, circa 1960.

A pie plate makes a good "operating room" for diagnosing and curing carburetor ills.

In any event, the points/contacts looked clean and smooth, although we ran fine sandpaper through them and made sure they were properly gapped at the open position. However, simply eyeballing the condenser revealed nothing. For diagnostics, a small-engine/outboard motor-ignition tester did its thing, fingering the condenser as being dead. Sure enough, replacing it with a new one enabled the system to generate a spark somewhat reminiscent of those scientific instruments in old black-and-white Frankenstein movies. That meant the coil and heels were fine where they were, so we took a moment to clean them up and then moved on to taking off the spring/inertia governor assembly, making sure we clearly understood how each of its intricate pieces was supposed to go back together again. Here, as in all of the engine projects, we snapped quick digital pictures so we could easily refresh our memories if things looked foreign during the rebuild.

Every small-engine redux involves deciding how far one should go with the project. Will it simply be a mechanical clean-up/fix-up, a revitalization that also gives the motor a bit of cosmetic work, or a full restoration to showroom quality? Because the Lawn-Cruiser struck me as being happily representative of the golden days when the Space Age and suburban living all seemed to come together in a naïvely

We dropped the float bowl and were pleased that it and the (cork) float assembly looked serviceably clean. Still, the parts were treated to carburetor cleaner. When working properly, the float responds to a full carb bowl of fuel by rising and pushing a fuel shutoff pin positioned above its pivot point. That long needle valve increases (when screwed open) or decreases (when turned downward) fuel flow so as to add or reduce fuel to the air carrying it to the combustion chamber. While this mill isn't one of them, some small engines have no user-adjustable needle valves, as they're internally preset at the factory.

wonderful way, I thought it deserved a restoration. That meant we'd go further than just getting it to run.

After inspecting things via taking off the magneto-plate/top main bearing/oil-seal assembly, we decided to leave the still well-performing crankshaft, connecting rod, piston, crankcase, and cylinder intact. All would need to be thoroughly cleaned with solvent.

Commercially available carburetor cleaner (spray) assisted in the carb rebuild, conveniently done in a disposable pie tin. Paint remover played a crucial role in taking certain pieces down to bare metal and readying them for respray in the closest-to-original green hue that could be found at the local auto parts store. (The best way to match paint is by taking the least faded part to the store to seek a corresponding color that satisfies your comfort level for detail. Few small-engine manufacturers had a dedicated replacement paint number/name system, as do automakers and outboard factories.)

Even with the paint remover, the cleaning process required a lot of handwork with sandpaper, wire wheel, and steel wool. Remnants of the latter are a real dickens to get out of certain places, like the flywheel magnets and between the cooling fins. Though a magnet more powerful than the magneto's might, in theory, help here, most small-engine mechanics admit that picking out (with fingers or tweezers) steel wool hairs from mags or blowing them away from nonmagnetic areas is the most effective process.

Following the fabrication of a few replacement gaskets and sharpening the mower blade, everything went back

The magneto with points cover removed appears to be functional, but its condenser got a "no good" rating from our trusty old Stevens ignition tester. Condensers can't be fixed, so a reminder to buy a replacement goes on our workshop clipboard.

As soon as a new condenser was secured, we mounted it and then reinstalled and adjusted (with feeler gauge and screwdriver) the points to open as wide as the OMC specifications indicated.

This tiny sponge in a holder next to the ignition coil heels gets treated to a drop of oil, allowing it to lubricate the cam that moves the points open and closed.

CASE STUDIES

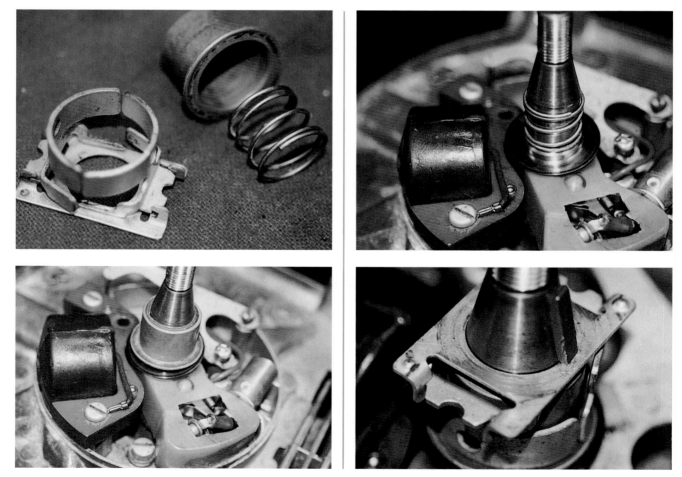

Perhaps the trickiest parts to get back together—properly fitted on the crankshaft top and held in place by the flywheel key—were those comprising the centrifugal governor assembly. Fortunately, we had the parts diagram to follow . . . and collective patience for about a dozen attempts.

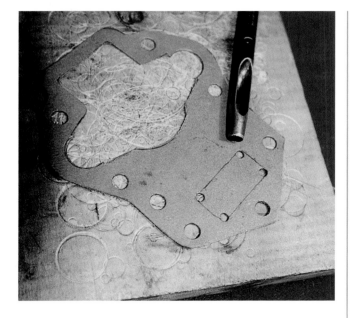

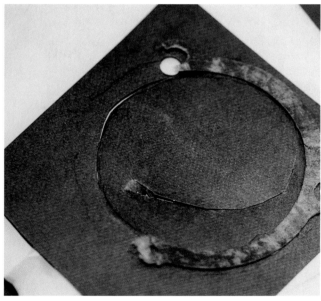

Can't find official factory replacement gaskets for your restoration? As long as it's not for a head gasket that requires a sheetmetal-sandwich center, gaskets can be cut from gasket paper available at an auto parts store. The hole-punch tool shown really beats trying to cut holes with scissors.

Using all that's left of an old gasket and the surface it came from, trace a new gasket.

Almost, but not quite good enough. The new gasket doesn't cover the mating area completely enough to serve its purpose. We had to make another one.

Every removed fastener and part should be cleaned and placed in a labeled bag or container to await reassembly. A dedicated piece of notepaper with reminders and hints about the nuts' and bolts' home is evident here.

Whenever a decal is at least 50 percent there and especially if no exact replacement is readily available—it's a tough decision whether or not to remove it. In the Lawn-Cruiser's case, we opted to strip it and the rusty spots poking through using paint stripper, rubber gloves, a dedicated brush, and a container.

Our first application seemed a flop . . . until we noticed that the instructions on the can indicated warm weather was better than subzero temperatures for facilitating the desired chemical reaction. Waiting until a sunny day did the trick, as this shot of application number two shows.

What to do with that nasty crack in the mower deck? We decided on a metal strap, bent to fit and bolted through the deck.

Drilling through the desired spot on the magnesium deck (above) was an exercise in patience, even after we made a "starter dent" with a prick punch.

After smoothing the repair with sandpaper, applying a touch of auto body filler, and doing a quick spray-paint test, the repair was complete.

After paint removal with chemicals and a date with the wire wheel, the motor cowling received fresh spray paint. The inside had already been brush-coated with primer.

Would you believe the Lawn-Cruiser's blade was dull and on backwards? No matter, the grindstone prepares it for a future on the "cutting edge" of mowing.

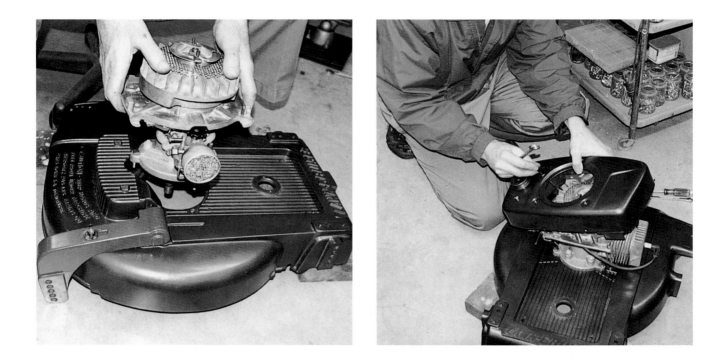

Cleaned, checked, and fit with a new condenser, the 2-horse OMC powerhead is reunited with its deck (above left). Following reinstallation of its fuel tank, the freshly coated cowling tops off the engine nicely (above right). At first, the rewind starter bolts wouldn't fit into their threads, so we used a tap tool to clean them of paint and a bit of stubborn stuff that hadn't been completely eradicated in an earlier application of gasoline (below).

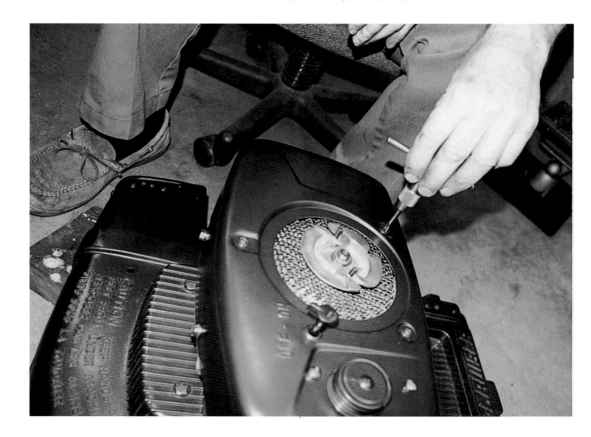

together successfully, with only one trip to the computer to consult a digital picture showing which way the wheels and handle brackets went on.

When the restored Lawn-Cruiser arrived in the front yard for a photo opportunity, some curious neighbors pronounced the vintage machine "too beautiful to use." I chuckled at their declaration, but after mixing some ½-pint-to-the-gallon fuel, gassing up the classic engine, and hearing it come to life on the third pull, I didn't have the heart to dirty it with grass clippings. Every once in a while, though, on the occasional sunny blue-sky afternoon, the mower's little Lawn-Boy model C-12B can be heard purring contentedly in my driveway. That 2-horse hum probably sounds just like it did on some idyllic, long-forgotten 1960 weekend in Ontario.

There's supposed to be a sediment screen on the inside of this fuel valve, but it was eaten away and an original replacement proved elusive. Instead, we used a universal inline filter available at small-engine shops and auto parts stores.

OMC dealers in Canada were authorized to identify used engines (Evinrude/Elto/Johnson outboards, Lawn-Boy and private-brand OMC lawnmowers, and Pioneer chainsaws) that were officially reconditioned with an "approved for resale with a new motor warranty" tag. The Lawn-Cruiser restoration team couldn't resist fitting ours with one for the mower's twenty-first-century debut. When my neighbor noticed me wheeling the now-restored version into the backyard for a few "after" pictures, he wondered if the Lawn-Cruiser might be for sale.

Before obtaining an illustrated parts list for our Lawn-Cruiser's C Series OMC Lawn-Boy engine, we plugged along with this graphic from an earlier Iron Horse A motor. While there were some similarities, the correct literature truly made things easier to decipher.

BUILDING A 1960s FOUR-CYCLE EDUCATIONAL POWER KIT

Most motor experts agree that a great way to learn small-engine repair is to find an ailing mill and take a shot at trying to get it going again. If the thing comes your way as a basket-case freebie, there's little to lose, even through the most uninformed experimentation. Of course, some wise instruction and experienced advice would benefit any small-engine student. That's why readers of magazines like *Popular Mechanics* have long been exposed to ads from home-correspondence schools offering to teach people small-engine repair for proverbial "fun and profit." The November 1978 issue of *Mechanix Illustrated* contains an example. "Earn extra cash income working right at home in your spare time or full time as a small engine repair expert!" an advertiser promoting its mail-order course promised. "Long before you complete your studies," the advertiser predicted, "you'll begin earning money on minor tune-ups and repairs. If you can read, you can master this craft with our hands-on training." Along with a notebook filled with lessons, some factory service manuals, and a small assortment of tools, the postal curriculum was shipped with a genuine 3½-horsepower Briggs & Stratton engine. Competing correspondence educators hawked similar study materials, but—depending on which engine maker would cut the school the best deal—their coursework came with different brand motors.

Upon noticing a "vintage Clinton NRI School *Power On Training* kit" on eBay, I figured the item would provide a rare opportunity to assemble a brand-new, 3½-horse, four-stroke mill decades after it might have otherwise already worn out and been relegated to the metal recycling bin. The seller knew little about the unbuilt motor's past, except that he'd found its sundry parts in a rather squashed and damp cardboard box on the last day of a Montana garage sale. Remarkably, all of the pieces were still present, except for a valve tappet and the carburetor, which probably got snatched long ago to patch up someone's ailing snowblower engine. Unfortunately, though, the only accompanying documentation was a glossy decal sticker touting the correspondence school's logo and indicating (in very small letters) a Clinton provenance. No model designation could be found on the crankcase/cylinder block, nor was an exact visual match noted in a thick Clinton master parts and service manual. Those anticipated three-ring binders filled with "detailed and easy-to-follow step-by-step build-it-yourself" directions were elusive, too.

Looking back, our educational kit engine assembly crew truly got the chance to learn from scratch on this project.

Magazine ads like these were crafted to coax people to pay tuition for correspondence courses in small-engine repair. Advanced curriculum included an actual educational engine kit like our Clinton mill.

"THERE'S OIL IN THEM THAR ENGINES! . . . I HOPE"

It would be nice if we could truthfully state that "motor oil is motor oil, so all motor oils are pretty much alike" and then go on to another topic. But such a declaration is far from accurate. Unfortunately, the fallacious assumption that oil doesn't much matter has made life miserable for many a poor little engine. Oil is assigned to the task of cooling as well as lubricating. One power-equipment repairman told me he's seen overheated four-stokers with transmission fluid in the crankcase. ("Well, the tranny fluid can was the same shape as a motor oil can," the owner reasoned when hearing the diagnosis.) The same engine doctor also recalls receiving ailing two-cycle mills with signs of too little oil in the fuel mix and, on the other side of the spectrum, plenty of plugged-up gas tanks and filter screens because the owners slopped a heavy-handed tip or two of oil directly into the tank.

Sand-cast onto the fuel tank of this 1949 Power-Pak mower engine are vital instructions that the moving parts in every two-stroke mill hope will be obeyed!

Key to a good two-cycle fuel blend is a dedicated container (indelibly marked "GAS/OIL MIX") in which oil is added to gasoline and both can be vigorously shaken together. It's a good idea to agitate this mix immediately before pouring it into the engine's tank. I know a Lawn-Boy collector who faithfully jiggles his mower a bit before starting it. "That way, everywhere there's gas, there's ample lubrication," he preaches.

There are wide differences in two-cycle oil. Besides viscosity (oil thickness) ratings, two-stroke lube is typically made with either "hot" or "cool" running engines in mind. The former typically includes air-cooled mills, while the latter covers water- (or other liquid-) cooled powerheads such as outboards. Speaking of two-cycle

Though the cans are all labeled with the likes of "Two-Cycle Oil," those on the ends are for chainsaws while the inside trio is meant to lube outboard motors. Air-cooled mills like saws, leaf blowers, and weed whackers run hotter than water-cooled outboards. The different blends take heat range into consideration while aiming for maximum lubrication and minimum carbon build-up

It's not that green two-cycle oil is better. When mixed with gasoline, its increased anti-friction effectiveness results purely from the color dye signaling that lube is present in the fuel, making it OK to start the engine.

marine engines, their oil has a "TC-W" (two-cycle, water-cooled) rating, as opposed to two-stroke oil for small air-cooled powerplants like those on trimmers, chainsaws, leaf blowers, and Lawn-Boy mowers. As a convenience for two-cycle motor owners, oil companies began dying their lube (typically red or green) so that a gas/oil mixture looks obviously different than straight gasoline. This "visual check" aspect has undoubtedly saved more than a few two-strokers from accidental operation with insufficient lubrication.

Oil working to reduce friction in a four-stroke engine spends a good portion of its effort radiating engine heat to the crankcase and cylinder block, where it can dissipate into the outside air. That means on a really hot day, or when the crankcase oil level is low, engine cooling and friction reduction suffer. Dirty oil cannot perform well in any environment because it has either lost some of its viscosity, contains grit (possibly metal particles from engine components), or both. This junk can scuff up internal parts. The resulting worn cylinder and piston surfaces then allow oil to "blow by" the piston rings and get into the cylinder combustion area, where it makes smoke and unduly carbonizes the cylinder, head, piston, spark plug gap, and valve mechanism.

Remove the cap nut from the crankcase pipe on this 9-horse Briggs & Stratton overhead valve snowblower engine and the oil will flow out.

When changing the lubrication, use quality detergent oil of SAE 30W (weight or viscosity) during the mowing season. If the oil you're perusing has a labeled service rating, seek SF, SE, SD, SC, or Better. Synthetic oil has its share of devotees in the small-engine community. Because there are so many ambient conditions, engine sensitivities, and oil specification ranges (such as the seemingly ubiquitous 10W-30), consult your owner's manual or ask the local small-engine repair shop person for advice on what's optimum for your particular application. No matter which oil is selected, it can be introduced as follows:

After running the engine for several minutes (to warm the oil), remove the drain plug (usually either on the crankcase bottom or side) and direct the lube into a container. If your engine is on a lawnmower and the plug is on the underside, requiring you to reach up past a blade to remove it, be sure to disconnect the plug wire! Replace drain plug. (You'd be surprised how many times this step has been forgotten!)

Some sources suggest filling the crankcase with kerosene, sloshing it around to loosen dirt in the crankcase area, and then draining it away. Others brand this as sort of a lazy person's overhaul technique, or consider it overkill.

Refill crankcase with fresh oil up to the "full" mark.

Start the engine and let it idle for a minute, and then cool it down for another minute.

Check oil level again. Fill to "full" mark if dipstick or crankcase indication line warrants.

If there's any universal fitting on small four-strokers, it's the little plastic oil-fill cap with those two protrusions that can be loosened or tightened with a screwdriver blade positioned sideways. More than a few of those "ears" have been sheared off by impatient folks who thought they were loosening when they were tightening.

It's important for two-cycle-engine owners to mix gas and oil in a container other than their motor's fuel tank. Whether it's a two- or four-stroker, introducing fuel into the tank by way of a funnel fitted with a fine strainer should ensure a clean drink for your machine. If not certain about a two-cycle engine's specific gasoline/oil diet, mix ½ pint of two-stroke oil per gallon of gas. Even if the oil container says 50:1, 100:1, or whatever ratio, use the ½-pint-to-a-gallon recipe (16:1) when unsure whether or not your mill has frictionless (or ball/roller/needle) bearings capable of coping with less lube than plain bearing motors.

Here's what came in the mail from an eBay online auction seller: as promised, a new-old-stock four-stroke Clinton engine kit from the 1960s.

The components were segregated into system groups on newspaper spread on the workshop floor. Doing so is the best way to see what you've got to work with.

Even though the parts were unused, decades of dubious storage necessitated cleaning of rust spots and mud dauber (wasp) dirt.

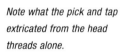

Note what the pick and tap extricated from the head threads alone.

The wire wheel is used to rid the crankshaft and camshaft of surface rust.

Lots of oil was applied to the piston before inserting it into the cylinder.

A ring-compressor was used to squeeze the piston rings so they'd clear the cylinder top. Here, the compressor is well lubed and loose enough around the piston to allow motion.

The connecting rod appears in the crankcase as the piston descends.

Even with the guide pins on the connecting rod end cap, it's still possible to put it on the rod backwards. Be aware of this, but don't feel alone if you ever inadvertently do so.

To ensure that the end-cap bolts don't wiggle loose during engine operation, Clinton used this tab to be bent onto the sides of the bolt heads and keep things in place. Other firms employed various lock washers or wire that ran through holes in the bolt heads.

The crankshaft is in place and secured to the piston/connecting rod/end cap/oil paddle assembly.

The camshaft is dropped into place and its timing mark matched with the corresponding one on the crankshaft gear.

Although having just completed reconstruction of a similarly formatted horizontal-shaft Briggs & Stratton mill, we were worried when the Clinton's crankshaft didn't initially appear to fit in the usual (or Briggs) way. Turned out, things were being inserted backward. It was then decided that a bed of newspaper on the basement floor should serve as a starting place where all of the components could be laid out in logical groupings: piston with rings, connecting rod, end cap, oil paddle, and related washers and bolts. Being able to see what we had to work with not only made finding corresponding parts easier, but also forced us to deal with mystery pieces whenever something didn't seem to fit just right. Our goal was to end up with no leftover parts and not to be missing any, either.

Concentrating on one assembly step at a time minimized frustration. For the first, we inserted the readied piston/connecting rod into the cylinder. Being new and springy, its piston rings were best coaxed into submission by way of a ring compressor that, when profusely oiled, helped the piston slide into place. Next, the crankshaft was fitted into the crankcase (and a main bearing) and onto the open end of the connecting rod. Admittedly, this took several tries. More fiddling resulted when we obeyed Murphy's Law and inadvertently installed the end cap backward. It sure looked OK, but didn't quite snug into the little notches on the connecting rod that ensure it can only go the right way. The goof was evident as soon as we tried rotating the crankshaft, and noticed the end cap bang against the crankcase wall. Happily, the valve tappets, valves, valve springs, valve-spring retainers, and valve keepers all cooperated when the camshaft was dropped into its intended crankcase home. Nuts! We forgot to line up the crankshaft and camshaft timing marks, and so went through the aforementioned routine again. Just for fun, we used a feeler gauge to measure the intake and exhaust valve clearances. Amazingly, they were within spec—had things been out of kilter, no easy adjustments would be available. This Clinton's valves, like those in many basic small engines, would have required precision machining and grinding to make them open and close just right. Often, when attempted at home by novice machinists, the surfaces aren't ground precisely, which introduces even more valve action (or inaction) trouble.

With all of the major moving parts in place, the four-stroker's crankcase was ready to have a gasket and its crankcase cover attached. When oiled in preparation, the other main bearing and seal slid cozily over the power end of the crankshaft and was buttoned up with some waiting bolts from one of the many little manila envelopes that Clinton originally supplied with the engine kit. A twist of the crank verified that everything was moving correctly. We were also visually

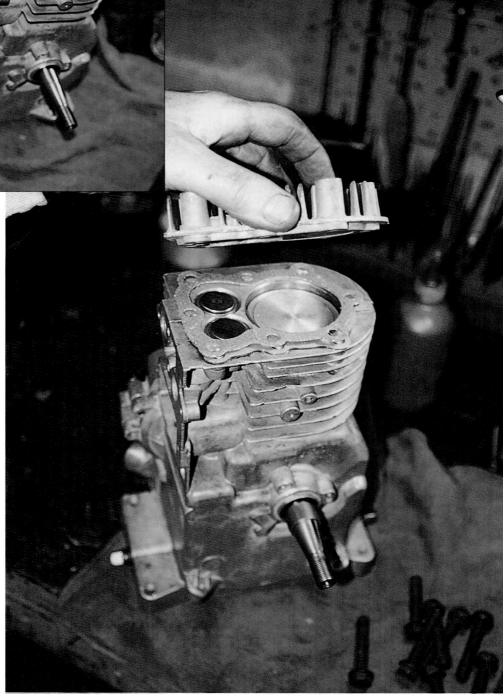

The crankcase is closed up (via its cover on the other side) to await installation of the valves . . .

. . . and cylinder head.

The head bolts are threaded down to their point of contact with the head and then torqued or tightened to factory specifications. If you don't have a manual detailing torque specs (or if you don't have a torque wrench), snug down bolts a bit past finger tight, but don't go so far as to strip the threads. Head-bolt tightening order is also covered in factory service manuals. The typical rule of thumb is to tighten bolts in an "opposite sides" pattern, as opposed to going around the head and thus ending up with a slightly tilted head.

satisfied that the valves popped up and descended nicely, so we bolted down the cylinder head and related gasket. Darn it! Another premature step! The cowling was supposed to be suspended from the head via four of the head bolts we'd just tightened in sequence. That meant the team earned a second chance to break in those new threads.

We soon discovered the red shroud couldn't go on yet, anyway, until the magneto and flywheel were mounted. With nothing in the spark plug hole to cause compression,

the eager "training kit" students clipped *The Small-Engine Handbook*'s official homebrew spark tester into place, spun the cast-iron flywheel, and cheered at the sight of a snappy flash. After some celebratory soda, we were revived with sufficient enthusiasm to mount the cowling and plastic gas tank. "She looks pretty good," came our assessment, though neither I nor my correspondence-school classmate will be eligible for a final grade on this project until a carburetor for the Clinton "training kit" can be located.

"Mag in a bag." Just prior to installing the flywheel, the magneto has to be fitted over the crankshaft end and secured to the crankcase exterior so that the coil heels can ride inside the flywheel and interact with its magnets.

Oh, boy! The flywheel fit and the mag (after we fasten the spark plug wire) works! Our Clinton kit is sitting in a galvanized small-engine repair pan primarily meant for four-strokers. That way, if crankcase oil leaks, it won't go all over the workbench and floor.

"If I only had a carburetor," the little Clinton might sing after being put together for the first time after spending 40 years as a bunch of parts, and then getting a whiff of the brisk October morning. She could probably use a rewind starter, too, but only the rope-start sheave came with this kit. The mascot on the vintage Tecumseh sign seems to be looking at his former competitor's engine with polite approval.

REVITALIZING A CURBSIDE JUNKER: 1990s MTD YARD-MAN

My wife and I have a kindly old family friend who worries too much about everything. When Carol mentioned to him that I was only a week away from this book's delivery deadline and hadn't yet had time to find a discarded lawnmower to chronicle, he nervously put out the word for one. I felt terrible turning down the dozens of his acquaintances who gladly offered me a wide assortment of infirm, rusted-out, and/or surplus mowers taking up space in their various backyard sheds. "No offense meant," began my appreciative explanation, "but in the spirit of some 'before and after' TV reality show, I have to find a truly downtrodden orphaned lawnmower/small-engine combo that's been wheeled to the curb on trash day. And there's no need to worry," I calmly pledged, "because we'll stay one step ahead of the garbage trucks tomorrow and be able to pick from a huge assortment of our community's finest junked mowers." At a little past eight the following morning, my thoughtful friend was simply worried about whether or not we'd selected the best one.

Truth be told, we stashed four wayward lawnmowers in the fellow's Ford F-250 pickup and had a tough time deciding which engine would get this book's makeover. After rejecting two of the group because their respective blade-brake mechanisms had been rather clumsily owner-defeated, we tossed a coin between a 1970s mystery brand powered by the representatively generic Briggs & Stratton Classic 2½-horse mill and a newer (1990s) high-rear-wheeled push mower fitted with a Briggs specially produced

"One person's trash is another person's Small-Engine Handbook *project." The paraphrased old expression turned out to be true with this 1990s Yard Machines walk-behind outfitted with a Briggs four-stroke mill.*

After testing for spark, project associate Lowell Foster shines a flashlight into the spark plug hole for a quick look at the piston crown and cylinder bore.

With the overall plastic shroud removed, the Briggs shows signs of grime from an oil leak or oil blow-by from the exhaust.

for Yard-Man. When the newer machine won the flip, I wanted to try again, but my buddy convinced me that the engine's relative youth would complement some of the vintage motors discussed elsewhere in the book. He chuckled that the MTD (Modern Tool & Die) Yard-Man already looked to be in better shape than his regular mower and recalled me promising that he could have whatever one we revitalized. I acquiesced and we rolled the Yard-Man into the small-engine hospital for diagnosis. After chasing away several daddy longlegs and more dangerous-looking spiders living under the plastic engine shroud and vacuuming the powerhead, here's what our workshop clipboard noted:

After the rewind starter and associated shrouding are lifted, instant evidence of leaf, lawn, and "mouse house" debris appears under the ignition coil and coil heels and in between the cooling fins. Clogged fins contribute to overheating that in turn minimizes the oil's effectiveness.

The cylinder head "as found" on the Briggs. Check out that oil and carbonization. Part of the problem was that the head bolts were loose. Much of the "glop" was removed with the wire wheel.

How's that for a gummed-up, carbonized valve? That oil trail at the head end of the cylinder bore is a sign that lubrication has gotten past the oil-control piston ring.

Some sandpaper cleans the head of the valve sufficiently for it to properly seat whenever the cam calls for it to descend. Be careful not to get grit into the valve seat and valve guide areas.

After cleaning and reassembling the cylinder head, valves, recoil starter, and shrouding, we bring the machine outside for a quick starting test (using starting fluid) without the carburetor. Admittedly, the team should have rid the mower deck of dirt and clippings prior to this over anxious step.

Here's what the dismantled air filter looked like before the dirt on the filter element was rinsed away in some gasoline. If not regularly cleaned, it can choke off air to the carburetor.

The rubber diaphragm on the lower right cavity of this carburetor base/gas tank assembly appeared to be stretched and loose, but worked fine after the unit was cleaned and put back together.

Spark is good, but spark plug is very dirty and oily.

Significant oil scatter on outside of (exhaust-side) crankcase.

Poor compression.

Loose bolts, indicating we weren't the first to investigate this B&S.

Upon removing the cylinder head, we noticed dirt and carbon buildup around both valves' heads, margins, and faces. The piston crown was carbonized, too.

The carburetor primer appeared to work properly, squirting gas into the carb throat with every push of the rubber button.

We cleaned the piston crown with a sharp chisel and treated the valves to some sandpaper, the latter allowing for improved valve seating. The cylinder bore looked factory smooth, though oil splotches trailed the piston when traveling down toward the crankcase. It could be that the oil ring was functioning aggressively, or maybe the rings were lodged in their seats and letting oil by too easily. Stuck rings could also explain the weak compression. Following treatment on the wire wheel brush, the head and its now-clean gasket were refitted to the cylinder. Compression was still less than stellar, but we decided to check the carburetor and think about a possible piston-ring replacement later. Some of the intricate carb components showed signs of rust and corrosion.

With the diaphragm removed, the carb cavity is visible. It had to be freed from some rust and corrosion partially blocking vital passageways.

The underside of the carburetor/fuel draw/primer unit that fits into the carb cavity built into the gas tank. We checked its screening for obstructions and found just enough blockage to warrant several shots of carburetor cleaner and some compressed air to "blow out the lines."

Wow! Does this need a bath or what? And we gave it one before re-mating this carburetor/gas tank unit to a receiver neck on the engine block. Note the dirt around the carburetor throat. We eventually realized that a protective O-ring that is supposed to be placed in the inner diameter of the throttle-body opening was missing, allowing significant excess air into the fuel vapor and lessening the crankcase's ability to pull fuel from the carburetor.

See that crankcase fuel intake neck? That's where the carburetor mounts. It is held tight by one bolt that also serves to hold the tank to the block. Ideally, the carb is sealed to the neck with the aforementioned O-ring. In many other engine designs, two bolts hold the carb to the intake on the block.

Cleaned, rebuilt, remounted, and treated to a new O-ring, the carburetor (still temporarily sans its air filter) is refilled with fresh gas and given three pushes on the primer button, positioned directly in front of the air filter mount. All is set for a test of our quickly revitalized Briggs.

After getting rid of the crud as best as we could without soaking the parts in cleaning solvent or bead-blasting them, the carburetor was reassembled and affixed to the engine. A shot of starting fluid convinced the Briggs to start singing on the first pull. Our cheers were short-lived, however, when the engine died with its last whiff of the stuff. Could it be that it's not getting gas? Fuel aroma on the spark plug ruled out that possibility. That plug electrode was pretty oily again, meaning more oil than was normal passed into the combustion chamber. All kinds of complex theories were offered in response to the B&S running reliably on starting fluid, but not on the gas in the tank. It must have been 15 minutes into this deliberation that I happened to wonder if the gas in the tank was old. Poured into an erstwhile mayonnaise jar, the fuel showed obvious signs of containing water. Might bad gas be the main culprit on our balky small-engine find? Fresh brew did the trick! Even so, I expressed concern that the rings probably needed replacement. "Aw!" dismissed my friend as he enthusiastically grabbed the Yard-Man's push handle and began cutting the lawn, "You worry too much!"

HELPING A RETIRED KART MOTOR RACE BACK TO THE TRACK: 1960s WEST BEND MODEL 580–09 POWER BEE

For Don Saulsbury, his brother, and dad, kart racing was a family affair. During the late 1950s and early 1960s, the Rochester, New York–area trio enjoyed spare time together by keeping their kart engines competitive. Most every weekend (except in deep-snow season) they had great fun racing around the surprising number of kart tracks that had been quickly established by local karting clubs and small entrepreneurs riding the original kart craze.

Decades passed, and Don had long since moved into the vintage racing boat and outboard motor collecting hobbies. We were chatting about the nuances of some rare 6-foot hydroplane, when I happened to compare the little craft to a kart. That started Don reminiscing and piqued my nostalgic interest enough to ask him to keep an eye out for any old, "reasonably priced" kart frame that he might spot along his leisurely circuit of antique auto and machinery swap meets.

"Found one!" the subject line read in an e-mail he shot my way later that summer. "Had to pay $60 for it, but if you'll take it off my hands for that, I'll deliver the kart and throw in a nice surprise I found under a bunch of stuff in my dad's cellar."

The 1962 Kavalla Kart by Bentas Brothers Company of Chelmsford, Massachusetts, was built in a chicken coop that the tiny kart-maker converted into a factory. When discovered during the summer of 2004, it was "powerless," but found a nice mate in a retired West Bend Power Bee Model 580 engine. Admittedly, this couple needs lots of work to get back on the track.

The identification tag and racing exhaust stack came with the deal. Both are vital for a showy restoration. Note that the ID plate dubs the West Bend a "Featherweight." The Hartford, Wisconsin, company long held this descriptive service mark, though another trade name, Power Bee, became more prominent on its kart mills. Early Power Products engines were branded "Light-Weight" (vis à vis "Featherweight"), perhaps causing a bit of confusion among nitpicky consumers.

A bath in some gasoline and then a spray of PB Blaster penetrant got things initially cleaned and freed up.

DEALING WITH A STUCK ENGINE

Citing the millions of late-model small engines in existence, a friend of mine laughed at the thought of someone troubling themselves with some motor suffering from a piston seized in its cylinder. "Just tell your readers," he strongly suggested, "to find a different one!"

"But they'd be missing the enjoyable challenge of bringing a mechanical goner back to life," I protested.

"Aw, baloney!" he gestured, but consented to discuss the matter that resulted in the following steps for freeing up a stuck piston:

Take everything that'll come loose off and out of the basic block. Ideally, this should lead to a headless cylinder/block. Also desirable is a piston that's stuck closer to the top of its stroke rather than toward the bottom. That way, it'll have some potential downward travel room. Trying to tap the piston upward from the bottom is possible, though seldom as convenient. In the case of a four-stroker, if the camshaft can be removed, do so at this point.

Using something along the lines of a 30-pound kitty-litter pail, soak the block/piston in solvent. Favorite recommendations range from kerosene to beer. Some patient folks simply squirt penetrating oil on top of the piston a couple of times daily and wait for it to work into the cylinder walls. Whatever you select, be sure this stuff is used properly and in a well-ventilated area.

After the aforementioned solvent or lube has been given time to function, position a piece of wood on top of the cylinder and tap it with a hammer. For engines without removable cylinder heads, use a wooden dowel (or rod) to gain impact access through the spark plug hole. The object is to free the piston without damaging it or related components. The process should be one of tapping and hopefully getting even a slight movement of the piston, adding more solvent or penetrating oil, and repeating the process later. Refitting the flywheel and key to the crankshaft can be helpful in trying to inch forward and backward in the quest to rotate the crankshaft and move the stuck piston.

For two-strokers, there's the added conundrum of the piston rings hanging up on a port. A common reaction to slow going (or no motion at all) is to become aggravated and really smash down on the piston. While this has moved a few stubborn pistons, the method more frequently leads to busted parts and questionable language.

Remembering that freeing a stuck piston is often a slow but sure process, be satisfied with a little change per session. In many instances, it's only a curiously small amount of rust, corrosion, or whatever preventing the desired action. Resolve, also, that there's no such thing as introducing too much oil to the piston and cylinder while coaxing things to slide again.

Once the piston has been removed, inspect it and the cylinder walls for desired surface smoothness. A honing might be in the offing. Many buffs don't even consider reusing the old piston rings, because new ones of just about

With the camshaft (and, if possible, the crankshaft) removed, remaining components are in a good position to coax the stuck piston out of its cylinder.

It turned out that the rings on this big Tecumseh's piston were rusted to the cylinder walls. With several applications of penetrating oil and tapping on the piston top, however, the rust's grip was defeated, and the components could be accessed for cleaning.

any size can be secured from various suppliers. Some enthusiasts, however, have had good luck giving their old rings another chance if sufficiently springy, cleaned up, and not damaged.

It should be mentioned that not all stuck engines are seized in the piston/cylinder assemblies. There are instances of magneto coil heels impacting the flywheel, jammed rewind starters, and rusted crankshaft and connecting rod bearings preventing their related parts from moving. Then there was the time I took a chance on a stuck Lauson that had a distinctive rattle inside. Removing its crankcase cover instantly revealed the culprit: a pretty nice Proto-brand ⅜–⁵⁄₁₆ combination wrench lodged in the camshaft mechanism. Someone had worked on the motor and then buttoned her up without making sure all his tools were accounted for.

On the little vehicle's engine mount, Don had bolted an early-1960s West Bend Model 580-09 Power Bee racing mill (serial number 13066), a classy addition to the frame. Referring to the Offenhauser engine of Indianapolis 500 fame, *Mechanix Illustrated* said, "[The 580 is] the Offy of two strokes in being 'a lunger and a legger,' meaning its low end torque is terrific and it can really get out and stride. It is equally reliable." Instead of the usual three-port design, this motor was fitted with another pair of intakes, which caused enthusiasts to dub it the "580 Five-Port."

When the sun set on the Saulsburys' karting days and their equipment was sold, Don's dad decided to keep the West Bend because he felt "it was quite a motor!" After some 40 years of waiting, the "Five-Port" was about to get

It seemed like this flywheel puller would be able to do its stuff, but for some reason the screw holes in the flywheel had never been tapped or threaded. That meant the flywheel would need to be removed by way of someone holding it (and the engine) an inch or so off the workbench while another person delivered a hammer blow to the top of the crankshaft.

The transfer port cover (one of two extras) making this West Bend a unique five-port version of the 580) is about to be removed for the first time since Lyndon Johnson was president.

Under the hood are signs of the port being filed open a bit more than factory original to allow for greater fuel intake. Besides a couple of oil spots on the piston, things look darn clean. Note that the rings still have enough spring to be slightly outside of the ring groove, but not hanging up on the port.

The other end of the transfer port reveals part of the connecting rod end cap—and some symptomatic rust that'll necessitate complete engine dismantling.

Vital tools for an engine overhaul: pie plates and small plastic bags to segregate and store small parts otherwise easily misplaced. An organized and adequately accessible workspace is key to productivity. Incidentally, a 1950s lawnmower engine service booklet predicted such motors "will require a complete overhaul every three or four years . . . a good mechanic . . . having about nine feet of workbench space . . . can overhaul a single cylinder engine in approximately four to five hours."

back into shape for a date with its new kart mate. On my workbench, the Power Bee received a full examination. Moderate surface rust covered the cowl, though the West Bend decal survived. A real goner, however, was the spark—not a trace of the fire that had seen the little engine win its share of Kennedy-era kart-track competitions. Removing the flywheel to cure the Wico-brand magneto underneath didn't turn out to be easy doing by myself. Rather, it served as a reminder that the job is best done with someone holding the flywheel (and engine) an inch or so above the shop bench while another mechanic carefully delivers a precise blow to a "keeper" (or one that can be banged and marred if necessary) nut threaded on flush with the top of the crankshaft. The Power Bee's rusty exterior led me to assume I'd see ignition points that needed to bite some fine sandpaper or emery board. After 40 years of basement dwelling, the condenser didn't surprise me when it registered "bad" on the tester. A length of new spark plug wire and a plug

connector cap topped off this "mag job," resulting in the production of a reliable zap with even a modest spin of the refitted flywheel.

West Bend–branded covers on ports four and five seemed to beg for a checkup. Under the top bypass port "hood" I was delighted to see an incredibly clean piston and two skinny little rings that possessed lots of springiness, plus a bit of forward/backward wiggle motion in their respective grooves whenever the piston moved. Everything was bone dry. Maybe the complete lack of oil for all those years contributed to the crummy compression. I squirted in a shot or two of new-old stock 1950s outboard oil known for its viscosity. It would later offer enough of a seal to boost compression considerably after just several twirls of the flywheel.

While concentrating on the piston and cylinder, as seen through port number five, I nearly missed a sight that would later require me to dismantle the Power Bee for access to the crankshaft and connecting rod. Suddenly visible

The beautifully restored West Bend 580 is ready to be fitted to an equally nicely redone kart . . .

through the crankcase end of the bypass port whenever the crank's rotation lifted the rod cap into view was some serious rust. It was a telltale sign that other critical moving parts could likewise be rust-coated. Being a "full-jeweled" or ball/roller-bearing engine, the high-performance West Bend 580 Five-Port mill shouldn't have to tolerate even microscopic foreign matter when high-revving and hoping to resist the woes of friction. The Power Bee is a notable small engine, representative of high-end circa-1963 karting, and came as a serendipitous gift, so it was only logical to give it a complete restoration, rather than a quick cleanup/fix-up.

Part of the fun in redoing a vintage motor comes from communicating with folks tackling a similar venture. Typically, the information that gets traded regarding each other's workshop experiences adds to both restoration adventures. Often, the collaboration yields useful historical research, too, with at least one of the parties turning up some period service manual or advertising brochure that really brings the project to life. In my case, via the rearenginekarts.com and vintagekarts.com Internet sites, I crossed paths with 1960s karting buff Bob Kurkowski, who had recently spent several months getting his West Bend 580 into blue-ribbon condition. Like all great small-engine restorations, Bob's Power Bee (a Model 580-07 wearing serial number 11023) underwent piece-by-piece disassembly, cleaning, replacement of worn parts (such as the piston rings, condenser, and spark plug wire), repainting, and reassembly. To yield show-quality results, no step could be skipped. After the last bolt was fastened on Bob's West Bend, it met its waiting kart and began a new life racing in classic karting competitions, giving young motorheads something to wish for, and bringing back memories to spectators there.

. . . like this one! Bob Kurkowski collection

When that West Bend needs a rest, here's a ready-to-race 1960s Clinton A-500 mill for some fast substitute work.

QUICK CURES FOR A COUPLE OF CONKED-OUT CUT-UPS: CIRCA-1980 STIHL FARM BOSS AND 1970s HOMELITE MODEL 150 CHAINSAWS

My neighbor was sitting on a small stack of logs that had been dumped into his driveway that October Saturday morning. A can of gas, some two-cycle oil containers, and two chainsaws were lined up several feet away. Since installing a wood stove, he'd acquired a pair of saws just in case one broke down in the middle of firewood season. "Taking a break?" I wondered.

"Got no choice," the fellow replied dejectedly. "Neither of my saws will start." I volunteered to assist in making some quick repairs, and ran home to fetch my toolbox—and a camera.

Both his circa-1980 Stihl Farm Boss and Homelite Model 150 hailing from 1972 were quality machines that appeared well treated and still had good compression. Even though

they'd been bought used (one at a power-equipment dealership and the other at a lawn sale), it made sense to invest some time and maybe a little parts money into getting them buzzing again. Neither of my neighbor's machines had been used since the previous fall (and even then with admittedly old mix), so we started our session by getting rid of the remaining fuel in their respective tanks. When inspected with a small flashlight, the bottom of the Homelite's tank looked pretty gummy. A half-pint or so of fresh gasoline sloshed around in it for a while, and then dumped into an old coffee can, floated out some sediment and general glop that certainly hadn't been doing the engine much good.

Next, we tested the duo's sparks. Nice and bright on the Stihl, but the Homelite's looked a bit weak and intermit-

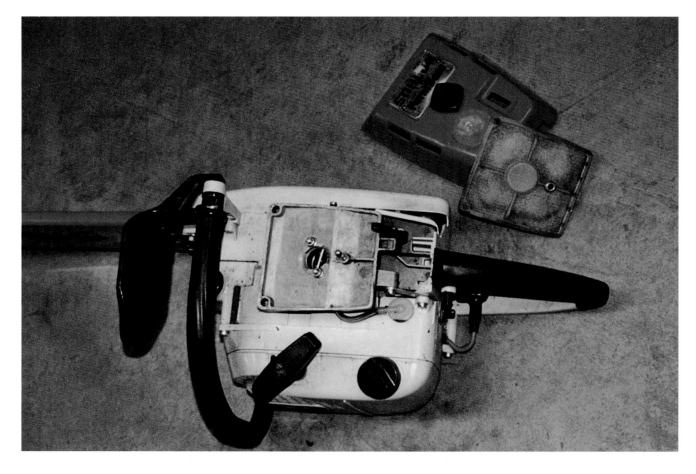

When an ignition checkup on this Stihl chainsaw didn't reveal why it ran so poorly, carburetion trouble was suspected. To gain access to the carb, the top shrouding and air filter were removed.

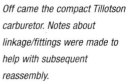

Off came the compact Tillotson carburetor. Notes about linkage/fittings were made to help with subsequent reassembly.

The carb-to-crankcase gasket didn't come off too cleanly. That throttle butterfly valve should be closed when the gasket residue is scraped down to the bare aluminum.

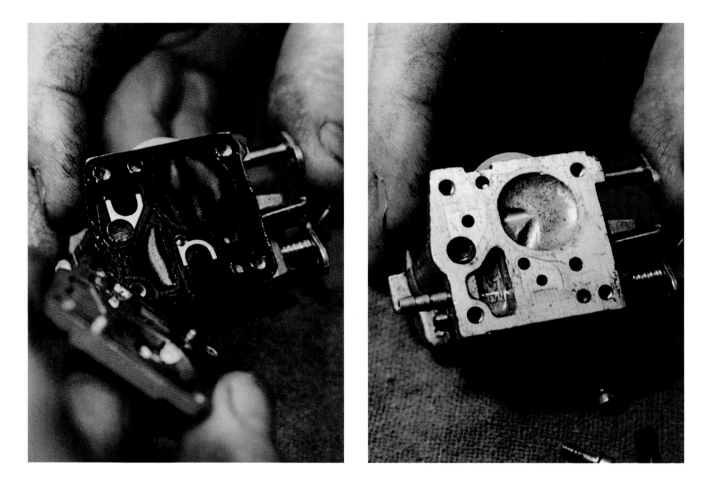

Unscrewing one of the carburetor side covers exposes the rubber-diaphragm "pump." These crucial sheets are prone to getting brittle and losing their oomph. After the diaphragm is removed, blow air into passageways to make certain they're free of obstructions.

tent. We figured a new condenser and possibly points would be needed, though we noticed a big improvement in the 150's fire after simply cleaning (or "dressing") its ignition contact points with an emery board nail file. Each saw had its spark plug treated to a cleaning with some sandpaper (for reconditioning the electrode and gap), de-rusting on a fine-wire wheel, re-gapping, and a blast of air from a compressor. Next, the saws' mufflers were removed to inspect for carbon or globs of oil obstructing the exhaust ports. OK in that department.

Checking off the aforementioned components led us to carburetion. We recollected that carbs, which must be able to meter fuel and air to an engine cocked at any angle, have little rubber diaphragms that serve as sort of a heart valve. These rubber valves are prone to drying out, due to age, heat, and long inactivity, and they become too stiff to build needed pumping pressure. As the Farm Boss is my compatriot's main chainsaw, he didn't hesitate to

head over to our local lawn and power-equipment shop to buy what is often called a "carburetor rebuild kit." The fresh gaskets, diaphragm, and tiny associated parts enabled us to methodically replace the suspect carb components with new innards and sure-sealing gaskets. Though the unique persnickety personality of many a small engine sometimes confounds even the most thorough revitalization, our quarter-century-old Stihl expressed no interest in an early retirement. Seconds after being closed back up, gassed up, and coaxed with a half-dozen quick, short pulls, it roared into action with such high-revving abandon that we didn't even feel a need to mess with the needle valves.

Could it have been that the little Homelite wanted to get out and play with his big brother? While my neighbor donned his protective goggles and commenced cutting firewood, I took another look at the 150. At first, I dismissed the good fortune that both saws might be cured that day,

The carburetor's other side is unveiled. Note the screw tops of the spring-steadied needle valve jets at center right. These should be removed and cleaned, and their passageways shot with air to ensure the channels are clear.

and envisaged the Homelite's troubles possibly being related to worn main bearings and/or bad oil seals. Resisting that complexity, though, I got back to basics and inspected the remaining obvious culprits: carburetion and an unobstructed fuel line passage from tank to carb. (Clean exhaust ports and acceptable spark were already givens.) The bright autumn sun threw shadows every which way in the engine compartment. One strategic tilt shot just enough light on the subject for me to notice that, even after refilling the tank and pulling the starter cord, fuel only made it partway through the line. We'd probably need to return to the small-engine shop for another carb kit, but my neighbor was busy sawing away, so I dumped the fuel (which again exhibited dirt and coagulated sawdust), sloshed the tank again with fresh gas, and then removed and cleaned the carburetor needle valves. Most motorheads who've fooled with one-lung, air-cooled mills admit that there's no official, common or "magic" needle-valve setting universally right for all small

engines—especially chainsaws! But I'd had good luck with starting places such as a ¼ turn of the seat for the idle adjustment and about 1½ turns from closed on the high-speed needle. I tried these on the 150, along with a shot of starting fluid I spied on a crowded shelf in my neighbor's garage. With full choke, the Homelite sputtered on pull number one and surprised me by starting up and keeping going via a second quick yank on its modest cord. When my neighbor saw blue smoke clouding from the 150, he put down the Stihl and happily yelled something over the collective racket.

"What'd ya say?" I shouted back, figuring he was probably insisting that I'd performed enough mechanical wizardry for the day and that his wife would treat us to some hot coffee and her famous apple pie. "That's great!" he exclaimed. "Now that we've got two saws running, you can get working on those small logs over there."

Here's what is typically dubbed a "carburetor (repair) kit," this one specifically for our Stihl's ailing carb. Contents include new gaskets and, in the case of this engine, a replacement diaphragm, passageway plugs, and a few other tiny parts that we decided did not need to be swapped out this time.

Carburetor cleaner in a pie plate did its thing before we fit the diminutive Tillotson with replacement diaphragm and gaskets. And, yes, even the semiprofessional small-engine revitalization team had to look at the instructional reminders jotted down earlier.

This cute little guy wasn't feeling too well. Crummy ignition, possibly due to a bad condenser or "frosted" (dirty/rusted) points, was the usual suspect, but a detailed spark/magneto test producing "great fire" ruled out that diagnosis.

CASE STUDIES

141

Maybe the exhaust port was clogged? Here's what we saw after removing the Homelite's muffler . . . A-OK.

How come the fuel isn't making it past midway through the line? Neither the cause nor the cure was very exciting: plain old dirty gas/oil that needed a thorough cleaning, and a fuel tank.

INDEX

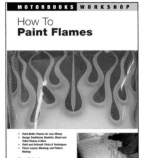

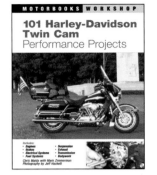